Pieces from the Past

Voices of Heroic Women in Civil Rights

Joan H. Sadoff, MEd., MSW, Editor

Co-Editors
Robert L. Sadoff, MD
Linda Needleman, MEd.

Tasora

ISBN 978-1-934690-47-5

Interior design by Kim R. Doughty
Design, typesetting, and printing by BookMobile

To order additional copies of this book, please go to:
www.itascabooks.com

Contents

Dedication

**To the women who changed the course of
history in this country—and the world**

To the Future

Jessie
Eric
Haley
Rachel
Jake
Azad
Maya
Cassidy
Jasmine
Bailey

Foreword

"What is most intriguing about . . . (these courageous women) is not that they suffered but that they stayed intact, human, and did not push their suffering down into another generation. This was true emancipation. I am left amazed at how many people did not let Mississippi destroy them or their spirits and amazed at how resilient humans can be, and that how they—as in the spiritual—can make a way out of no way."

—Anthony Walton, *Mississippi,* Vintage Books, A Division of Random House, New York, 1996, p. 274.

Preface

Joan H. Sadoff

*"It all connects. That's the first thing you need to remember, and the
last. Anywhere you start, you are walking into the middle of something.
There is no way you can go back to the actual beginning, because there is
no beginning and no end. History is not a straight line but a rolling wheel;
it's a perpetual story, and all the spokes of it eventually tie together."*

—John Egerton, "Speak Now Against the Day."
Alfred A. Knopf, New York, 1994

The spokes of the wheel go 'round and 'round—taking on speed, blur-
ring the past with the present. Time is a continuum, mostly linear,
punctuated by the never-ending blips, some more noticeable than others, always competing for place and space. The wheel of history, without
specific beginnings and endings, includes the stories of black and white
women who joined forces to confront the indignities and inequities of
their times. Their lives as students, homemakers, activists, parents, teachers, sharecroppers and attorneys reflect the demographic mix and multi-
ple generations. These women, who represented the racial, socioeconomic
and educational spectrum of their time, shared a sense of selflessness and
devotion to a cause much larger than any personal pursuit. They challenged themselves and others to force America to live up to her promise
of equality for all.

There were countless poor, unknown women throughout the South
who braved threats on their lives and the lives of their loved ones, loss of

employment for themselves and their families, for the cause of freedom. Bombings, beatings, lynchings, and burnings could not deter them. They had defined their moment and would not wait for the next generation to do their job. Their time was "NOW" . . . there was no turning back. White women who joined the cause found themselves facing their own set of challenges. Some were ostracized from their families while others were rejected and isolated from friends and communities. In the lists of women's names associated with civil rights history, there are more black women than white. Nevertheless, the white women who are recognized for their involvement and courage stand out as heroes for their service to the cause of humanity and freedom for all.

Colum McCann, author of "Let the Great World Spin: A Novel," reminds us that "not all life is already written down; there are still so many stories to be told."

"Pieces from the Past" is a collection of stories which reaches beyond the personal, that addresses the issue of a world that is larger than the immediate one in which we live. These are the stories of people who believed they could make a difference, that they could change the *status quo,* that they could make the world a better place. History will continue to record the stories of their heroism, their willingness to stand up for the civil rights of all people and to sacrifice their personal safety in the pursuit of freedom.

Through their courage and actions, we learned that fear can be challenged and that behaviors can change. As a result of their perseverance and dedication to achieving equality among the races, we now have a number of black leaders throughout the country and the election of Barack Obama, the first African American President of the United States of America.

"Pieces from the Past" resonates with the voices of women who exemplify the best of the human spirit. They describe their observations and insights through the experiences of daily life. They share their feelings, their hopes and dreams. They invite the reader to travel with them on their personal journeys, finding their way on the wheel of time. These women took to heart Horace Mann's words to the 1859 graduating class of Antioch College: "Be ashamed to die before you have won some battle for humanity."

These are the stories of black and white women who found their courage through the support and strength of those who came before them and worked to sustain the fight for the right to vote and to enjoy the same privileges as their white counterparts. These women are my heroes; they and their stories have inspired me and changed my life. Their message is irrefutable. They challenge us to continue the never ending battles for humanity and to honor those who preceded us. We stand on their shoulders—it all connects.

Introduction

Joan H. Sadoff

"Pieces from the Past" presents a unique approach to the civil rights era by linking known history to the faces of heroines during this pivotal time in American history. The stories told by these women, or about them by friends and/or relatives, provide the background, texture, composition and voice that keep the memories alive. The purpose of this book is to present a compilation of stories, each one unique to the individual and at the same time revealing the common threads that bind them together. Each essay serves as a model of individual strength and inspiration as well as a reflection of community solidarity in which the women worked together for a common cause. This book adds another spoke to the ever "rolling wheel" of history.

The Beginning

It was fall, 1991. After many years in the practice of clinical social work, I had decided to make a career change. I was looking for something new—something different—something which remained undefined until PBS presented a three part series on the JFK years. Unexpectedly, I found myself riveted to the television set as the second part of the series, which focused on civil rights during Kennedy's administration, came into view. I was unprepared for the archival footage which followed: the scenes of a busload of Freedom Riders outside of Anniston, Alabama, en route to Birmingham; the mob of white people, armed with baseball bats and clubs, waiting for the bus to come to a full stop; the bashing of windows and the torching of the bus; the bus riders attempting to extinguish the flames. These images haunt me to this day.

The history of Mississippi is replete with stories of slavery, segregation, poverty and the abuse and mistreatment of black people. Images of the KKK, murders, lynchings and the memory of three civil rights workers, Andrew Goodman, Michael Schwerner and James Chaney, who lost their lives in the struggle for civil rights, all hang in the gallery of that notorious era. There were women who participated in challenging the status quo politically, socially and psychologically; and others who sacrificed personal safety and security for the well-being of all. My response to this archival footage was visceral. My husband agreed to accompany me on a trip to Mississippi the following summer in search of people who had lived through and experienced this history first-hand. I needed to know more about the courageous people of Mississippi.

The Trip

It was August, 1992. The sign read, "Welcome to Mississippi: The Magnolia State." The intensity of the sun was mitigated by the abundant greenery which lined the highway. The road was flat and in good repair. Small, single dwellings dotted the landscape. Pick-up trucks, a rope swing, spare tires were common to the area. A reservoir, named after Ross Barnett, former governor of Mississippi, was a landmark with name familiarity.

August in Mississippi is typically hot, but that was not what I remember. What I do recall was the sense of uncertainty and the unrelenting question: "What am I doing here?"

Our plan was to talk to as many people as we could about their first-hand experiences during the civil rights period. We spoke to people in parks, gas stations, restaurants, bus stops, churches, on the steps of the courthouse, wherever and whenever we could. Initially, we had some reservation as to how we, as white Northerners, would be accepted and whether people would trust us with their memories. We asked the same questions over and over again: "Were you here during the civil rights movement? What was it like? Did you march with Martin Luther King, Jr.? What was it like? Did you choose not to march with Martin Luther King, Jr.? How did you make that decision? What was it like? What was it like? What was it like?" We spoke to white people, black people, older people, younger people, Catholics, Baptists and Jews. What we found was that everyone had a story they were willing to share! In addition to meeting people in Jackson, Mississippi, we were eager to visit the Mount Zion United Methodist Church near Philadelphia, Mississippi, where a memorial had been established in memory of Goodman, Schwerner and Chaney.

While driving on a deserted country road and unable to find the church, we stopped at a home to ask for directions. There we met Arecia Steele, who asked what we were doing and why we were looking for this church. When I told her, she asked if I had a tape recorder with me. She said, "I have so many stories to tell." A trip, initially planned to enhance our personal edification and understanding of Mississippi history and civil rights, was beginning to take on a new dimension. Mrs. Steele became a major player in leading us to others who would contribute to our future project. It was following our chance meeting with her that we decided we had to do something with these stories before the people died.

The Project

We returned to Philadelphia, Pennsylvania with a sense of purpose. Through a friend, I was referred to Joe Anderson, librarian at the Balch Institute of Ethnic Studies in Philadelphia. Our plan was to focus on Philadelphia, Mississippi, a town of six thousand people. It was the place where the bodies of the three civil rights workers were found. Philadelphia, Mississippi had name recognition and historical import. People noticed Neshoba County on license plates and knew that "something terrible" had happened there. The community was manageable in size with a relatively stable population. We planned to focus on the issue of change, asking people who had lived in Philadelphia, Mississippi before, during and 30 years post-civil rights, in their experience, what had changed, what had not changed and what needed to change in order for race relations to improve.

Joe Anderson confirmed that focusing on Philadelphia, Mississippi and the issue of change had not previously been documented and recommended we proceed with our plans for a documentary film. He referred us to Professor William Ferris, who was then director of the Department of Southern Culture at the University of Mississippi. Bill liked the idea and agreed to be our academic advisor. Through our children, we became acquainted with Garth Stein and Andrea Perlbinder, both recent graduates of Columbia University's Film School. They agreed that the Philadelphia, Mississippi stories needed to be told and they would help us by directing our project. My husband, Bob, and I returned to Mississippi to locate people who would be willing to participate in the interview process, recognizing that speaking privately and being seen on film are two very different experiences. Not everyone wants their neighbors to know what they are thinking.

The Middle

We arrived in Jackson, Mississippi to begin planning the format of what would become our first documentary film: "Philadelphia, Mississippi: Untold Stories." The Edison Walthall Hotel, in Jackson, was considered to be among the oldest hotels in the city. Built in 1928 and named in memory of Edward Cary Walthall, a major in the Confederate Army in 1864, and later appointed to serve as a United States Senator from Mississippi from 1885 to 1896, it stood as a remnant of the past as much as a reminder of the present. The hotel had been built less than a decade after thousands of black Americans left Mississippi and other parts of the South as part of the first Great Migration. They headed toward industrial cities such as Chicago, Detroit, New York and Philadelphia in search of a better life. The dream of access to a better education for their children, reasonable employment and a decent place to live were among the goals for these pioneers as they arrived at new and unknown destinations.

The formidable and painful history of blacks dating back to the 1600's in this country was with me as I opened the door to our hotel room. It was tempting to think about others who had occupied these rooms, their stories, their politics and their roles in Mississippi history. Our room was sparsely furnished and dimly lit while expressing a hint of musty air. In the corner was a small, simple wooden table, reminiscent of the Shaker style, which I would use for a desk. I stood in the doorway, taking in my surroundings and asking the questions which I now considered seriously: "What am I doing here? Where do I start?"

I decided to make contact with people recommended by Arecia Steele. She led me to Bud and Beatrice Cole, longtime residents of the Longdale Community and members of the Mount Zion Church. It was on the grounds of this church that Mr. Cole had been beaten by members of the Ku Klux Klan in June, 1964, after an evening service. Mrs. Cole had pleaded for her husband's life. When one of the Klansmen said it was too late, Mrs. Cole started praying and the beating stopped. The church was burned later that night. The following Sunday, three civil rights workers (Goodman, Schwerner and Chaney) visited the ruins of the church after which they were arrested and subsequently murdered by the Klan.

I continued making phone calls and meeting with people to get their stories. I found approximately fifty people who were initially willing to be interviewed for the film, but only thirty finally agreed to speak on camera. It is interesting to note how the decision making process often focused on concern about losing jobs and status in the community. There were those who were fearful of the social repercussions in this small town where change had come to some areas but where many parts were still racially segregated. In addition, there were those who met us on the street, telling us to put a good spin on their community, as it had previously been negatively portrayed in the national media.

Our Philadelphia, Mississippi odyssey led us to the offices and homes of many prominent Mississipians including Dick Molpus, Secretary of State; Bill Minor, award winning journalist for the Clarion Ledger, (Jackson); Florence Mars, author of "Witness in Philadelphia;" Tom Wacaster, Director of the Phil Hardin Foundation, (Meridien) and attorneys Fenton DeWeese and Constance Slaughter-Harvey (Forest). We met with and heard stories from Boots and Millie Howell (Philadelphia), Mickey Prim (Jackson), Al and Rhoda Herzog (Meridien), Goldie and George Hirsberg (Clarksdale),

Bea Gotthelf (Jackson), Pete Talley, Reverend Clinton Collier, Reverend Steve Mosley and Ellen Spendrup (Philadelphia). We shared meals together and spent time with extended families. We were reminded of the importance of revisiting the sites of trauma in our country, to mourn and then to move on. "Philadelphia, Mississippi: Untold Stories," a documentary film reflecting the stories of people who lived through the changes brought about by implementation of civil rights in Mississippi in the 1960's, was the recipient of the Bronze Award of the National Educational Film and Video Festival, 1995.

The Next Chapter

"Philadelphia, Mississippi" created an easy segue to "Standing on My Sisters' Shoulders," our next documentary film which tells the stories of courageous black and white women and their involvement in civil rights in Mississippi in the early 1960's.

Mississippi provided the perfect place to retell civil rights history for a generation of young people, many of whom are unfamiliar with this most significant era in our history. How many young people know that there was a time when black people were not allowed to walk on the same sidewalk as a white person? That black people were only allowed to shop on certain days, and that if they tried on an article of clothing they would have to buy it? Most people know about the segregated schools and the separate accommodations, including bathrooms and drinking fountains, and the lack of voting rights, but how many know that blacks were asked to answer impossible questions such as "How many bubbles are there in a bar of soap?" in order to show they were illiterate and therefore unqualified to vote? I didn't know that whitewall tires, popular in the 1950's, were not allowed in Mississippi because of the suggestion that black and white together was acceptable.

History typically has focused on the works of male leaders such as Martin Luther King, Jr., Medgar Evers, Ralph Abernathy and Bob Moses; few people know of the scores of women whose courage and resolve were the backbone of the movement.

In preparation for the production of "Standing on My Sisters' Shoulders", we conducted spontaneous interviews of a cross section of people representing different races and ages. We asked the volunteers to identify the names from a list of women who had been active in the civil rights movement. The list included Rosa Parks, Fannie Lou Hamer, Unita Blackwell, Annie Devine, Mae Bertha Carter, Diane Nash, L.C. Dorsey, Winifred Green, June Johnson, Dori and Joyce Ladner, most of whom were from Mississippi. The only name they recognized was that of Rosa Parks. Clearly, there were a significant number of "unrecognized" women who had made noteworthy and life changing contributions to the movement and to the future of this country. It was essential that their stories be told.

"Standing on My Sisters' Shoulders", which took 5 years to complete, was made possible by a staff of dedicated professionals, many of whom volunteered their time and expertise because they believed in these women and the importance of validating their work to ensure their place in history as courageous women of the 20th Century.

Women Make Movies, New York City, began distributing "Standing on my Sisters' Shoulders" in the fall of 2001. Almost immediately, an interest in the film surfaced and "Sisters" began finding its way into markets around the world. The film was shown in 28 film festivals, nationally and internationally, receiving 14 awards, including best documentary (Pan African Film Festival, Los Angeles, California and Pensacola Film Festival, Pensacola, Florida); Audience Award (for Dances with Films, Los Angeles, California and the Atlanta Film Festival.) More importantly, "Sisters" was being shown in classrooms from coast-to-coast to rave reviews. Students began writing papers about these women and sent letters to us praising their courage. Teachers described the impact on their pupils with the hope that the influence of the Mae Bertha Carters and Fannie Lou Hamers of this world would serve as models for the next generation.

In October, 2004, the Black Students Fund showcased "Standing on My Sisters' Shoulders" at the Kennedy Center in Washington, D.C. Almost all of the "Sisters" were able to attend and found themselves the recipients of a standing ovation, accompanied by an overwhelming expression of gratitude from those in attendance who applauded them for "standing up" and ultimately, making the world a better place.

Since the film was released, I have had the opportunity to address over 160 audiences representing all segments of society. Each time, for me, it is like "the first time" I showed the film. There is always an excitement, an anticipation and an opportunity for the viewers to share in the exchange of ideas about how people can make a difference in their lives and in the lives of others. "Sisters" is always fresh; "She" teaches history and utilizes personal experience. "She" grows wiser with the passing of time.

It has been 10 years since "Sisters" was first shown. I still marvel at the women, their stories and contributions to our country and to the world. Their achievements continue to resonate as they remind us daily that if you can envision something, you can make it happen.

Moving Forward

"Pieces from the Past" provides a new venue through which to highlight personal details of the lives of these extraordinary women. We are inspired by learning of their strengths and sacrifices which they demonstrated without hesitation. It was these women who risked their lives by providing places for the civil rights activists to meet with community members. They opened the church doors for meetings, they put food on the table for visitors and provided shelter for those who came South to help. It was these women who were on the front lines daily, making sure that the freedom to register to vote and, ultimately to vote, became a reality. Their contributions to the formation of the Mississippi Freedom Democratic Party (MFDP), (Fannie Lou Hamer, Annie Devine), integration of schools (Mae Bertha Carter and her daughter, Gloria Dickerson), the first black female graduate of the University of Mississippi Law School (Constance Slaughter Harvey) and the first female black mayor in Mississippi (Unita Blackwell) are well known. Some of these women were in the Winona County Jail (Fannie Lou Hamer and June Johnson) and sat in at the Woolworth's lunch counter in Jackson (Joan Mulholland). Their stories were selected from "Standing on My Sisters' Shoulders" for this book as supreme examples of courage and determination. The personal details of their lives, inner feelings and insights, found nowhere else, are featured in "Pieces from the Past."

We have been fortunate to have several of the surviving women write their own stories. Betty Pearson, in her late eighties, portrays her own experiences as a liberal white woman during the civil rights movement and her subsequent contributions following the civil rights era. Joan Mulholland depicts her role as a white Southern woman in the civil rights movement and her enrollment at Tougaloo College, an historically all black college, in order to demonstrate to black students that the struggle was not theirs alone.

Other stories are written by friends and relatives of these women who either have passed on or are unable to write their own. Some of the chapters have been written by prominent historians and professional writers, including Joanne Prichard Morris, Constance Curry, Monica Land, Bill Minor and Stan Dearman. Others are presented by relatives who share their relationships with, and intimate details of, the lives of these brave women. Hence, the chapters are uneven in length and style, but reflect the voices of these women in their own words or in the language of those who knew them best. The "Pieces" are all related to the character and traits of these women, depicting their courage, insights, strengths and weaknesses. Thus, the book is a mixture of "Pieces from the Past" that are tied together by a common thread: "It all connects."

Unita Blackwell

"I was beginning to figure out that we were on to
something bigger than I had ever dreamed."

*Unita Blackwell declared to all who would listen—"Nothin' from nothin'
leaves nothin', if I die, I die for somethin.'" She stood as a beacon of strength
and hope: a constant reminder that the goal of freedom was worth fighting
for! She was selected by Shirley MacLaine to join a group of women visiting
China for the first time. She was also named as a recipient of the MacArthur
Genius Award.*

JoAnne Prichard Morris

*JoAnne Prichard Morris was executive editor of University Press of Mississippi
from 1982 to 1997. She is the widow of Harper's Magazine editor, William
Morris. Currently she is senior editor of the Jackson Free Press. She most recently co-authored a book with Unita Blackwell: Barefootin': Life Lessons
from the Road to Freedom (2006), describing Unita Blackwell's incredible
life experiences. The book was published to high acclaim, winning a prestigious Christopher Award for "Affirming the highest values of the human
spirit." "I was privileged to work with her on this book, and I am proud to
call her my friend."*

Unita Blackwell and I both grew up in the Mississippi Delta in the days of segregation. Although we lived only sixty miles from each other, we inhabited two different worlds—worlds about as far apart as they could be. Mine was characterized by privilege and opportunity, Unita's by restriction, subservience and impediment. The sole qualification for membership in each was the color of one's skin. Unita and I both still live in Mississippi, but now we share the same world. Unita Blackwell was a significant force for bringing about the changes that made our shared world possible.

Unita expected to spend the summer of 1964 the same way she had spent nearly every other summer of her life—working in the cotton field. That's about all an African American could do in the Mississippi Delta, unless one were lucky enough to attend college and get a job as a schoolteacher. Unita had completed only six grades. She was thirty-one years old, living with her husband and a young son in the tiny unincorporated community of Mayersville on the Mississippi River in the most rural county in the state, "stuck in poverty and trapped by the color of my skin on a rough road to nowhere," as she wrote in Barefootin'. Even in the sweltering heat of summer, she'd be cooking their meals on a wood stove, pumping water outside to drink and to wash dishes and clothes and bathe in. She didn't have to worry about cleaning up the bathroom, though, because they didn't have one. Would they ever have a decent house in Mississippi? She doubted it. They had gone down to Florida to pick tomatoes and get rich, but that didn't happen; after a couple of years, they came back to Mississippi. Just thinking about her life made her weary. She desperately wanted something to give purpose to her existence. When she heard Martin Luther King preach on the radio or saw him on television leading a march, she dared to dream that change would come. But everybody knew that Mississippi would be the last place it would happen.

In the spring of 1964 the media reported that hundreds of students from the North would spend the summer in Mississippi registering black people to vote. They were part of the organization Student Non-Violent Coordinating Committee (SNCC, pronounced "Snick.") At that time only 20,000 black people in the entire state were registered to vote. Unita Blackwell was not among them. In fact, there was not a single registered black voter in Unita's county. Unita had never attempted to register. She had never participated in a civil rights activity. But when she heard whispers around Mayersville that some of the students might come there, she hoped it was true. Her friend Coreen warned her that getting involved with "Freedom Riders" could get her killed. "I don't know what difference it would make,"Unita said, "I'm dying anyway."

The whispers proved true, and when two black SNCC students came to her church explaining to the congregation that voting was their constitutional right and the key to a better life, Unita was among the first to volunteer. On a blistering June morning–not long after Goodman, Chaney, and Schwerner had turned up missing in Neshoba County— she was among a small group of local black people who appeared at the courthouse in hopes of registering to vote. As her group waited outside, the sheriff came by and warned, "It's against the law to stand this close to the courthouse."

In *Barefootin'* [1] Unita Blackwell describes the events that transpired and her own reactions to them:

> *The news whipped through Mayersville like a brush fire: A bunch of niggers over at the courthouse. Soon a gang of folks had gathered to see what we were up to. There were eight of us standing in a cluster by the side door of the Issaquena County Courthouse—me and my husband, Jeremiah, Mrs. Ripley, the Siases, and three schoolteachers. I probably stood out in the group since I'm close to six feet tall and near about as*

---

1 From "Barefootin': Life Lessons from the Road to Freedom" by Unita Blackwell and JoAnne Prichard Morris. Copyright 2006 by Unita Blackwell and JoAnne Prichard Morris. Reprinted by permission of Crown Publishers, a division of Random House, Inc.

black as a person can be. People hadn't ever seen anything like this in our little Mississippi Delta town—black folks didn't hang around the courthouse. Hardly any blacks ever had reason to go to the courthouse at all. And nobody was expecting to see it that morning. They could tell we weren't waiting for a ride to the cotton field, because we didn't have our loose ragged work clothes; we weren't all dressed up for church, either. We were dressed plain, but neat. We had come to register to vote. It's our right as Americans, the Constitution says so. We ain't leaving. I believe we'll just stay here until we get in to see Mrs. Vandevender.

Mrs. Mary Vandevender was the circuit clerk for the county, and she was the one who'd give the voter registration test to us. I knew about the test. I'd have to fill out a long application, read a section of the state constitution, and "interpret" it in writing. Whether you passed or not was left entirely up to the person giving the test. That was the law in Mississippi and that's the way black people had been kept from voting for years, if they ever got that far along in the process. The last time any blacks had tried to register in Issaquena Country was about 1950—two fellows who had come home from the Army— and they were turned away at the courthouse door.

We agreed that since Minnie Ripley was the oldest, she ought to be the first to go in. "Mother Rip" was in her seventies and had lived in Mayersville all her life. Everybody, black and white, knew her and respected her. She was a devoted church worker. She wasn't a very big lady, but she had a big presence about her and always a spring in her step, and she pranced right on into the courthouse.

We crossed the street to stand under a couple of big oak trees, and Sheriff Darnell ambled off. It was still fairly early in the morning, but the summer sun was already bearing down, and even with my straw sun hat on, I was glad to get in the shade. The grass was worn down under the tree and we hadn't had a sprinkle of rain in over a month, so the dust got all up in between my toes in those old slides I was wearing. I had no idea what I was in for, and I must have been anxious and tense, but today, at the age of seventy-two, I remember only how clear my mind was and how determined and strong I felt.

As soon as Mrs. Ripley went inside the courthouse and the sheriff left, Preacher McGee came hustling over to us. A wiry, light-brown-skinned fellow, he was what we call a "jackleg" preacher, one who doesn't have a regular church of his own. "Y'all need to get away from here," Preacher McGee said. Don't stir up nothing." He was nervous and talking fast.

We knew the sheriff—or some other white man—had enlisted him to convince us to leave. You always had black folks like Preacher McGee that did what the white men told them to. Some of them were scared not to. Others just wanted to pick up a dollar or two. I believe Preacher fit both of those categories.

Soon a bunch of white fellows started circling the courthouse in their pickup trucks. Guns were hanging on gun racks in the back window for all of us to see. This was the first time I ever saw guns displayed that way. Before the sixties, white men did not usually ride around town with a rack of guns in their trucks. You might have seen a gun every once in a while when the person was going out hunting deer or rabbits or something. That day we were the rabbits.

The men parked their pickups on the street around the courthouse, making a circle. There were half a dozen trucks, as I recall. They hollered at us from inside their trucks: "Niggers. niggers. Go home, niggers." The sheriff came walking back by again; by this time he had picked up his pace and was shouting at us: "Y'all go on home. Get on away from here." Preacher McGee kept walking around, twitching and pleading with us, "Come on, y'all, come on. They mad. Come on, come on. Y'all come on."

But we did not leave.

The men climbed out of their pickups and walked over to where we were standing. They brought their long hunting guns with them. I'd seen these men around town and knew who they were—farmers, most of them. They stopped right in front of us and stood there glaring. Nobody said a word. Their faces were bright red. I had never before seen that kind of rush of blood in a person's face. In those days a black person wasn't supposed to make eye contact with whites. But I looked right into the eyes of one of those white fellows. And he looked straight at me, and if eyes could have shot me down, they would have done it. Hate mooned out just like a picture.

I didn't know what was going to happen next or what I would do. I didn't have a gun or any other weapon to protect myself None of us did. SNCC believed in nonviolence, and we were following SNCC. I was frozen with fear.

Pictures were flashing through my mind: the three civil rights workers who had gone missing in Neshoba County just the week before; Medgar Evers, murdered the previous summer, shot in the back while his wife and little children watched; Emmett Till at the bottom of the Tallahatchie River with a cotton gin fan tied around his neck. I had learned about these violent acts soon after they happened, and others like them, and l knew they were true. But they had never seemed real to me until that day. I had never believed or accepted or understood that something like that could actually happen to me. From birth I'd been taught not to hate white people, or anyone, to work hard and treat people right, and to have faith that goodness would win out over evil and hatred . . .

But everything came together for me the day those white men with guns surrounded me at the courthouse. I could taste and smell reality. These white men—people I saw around town, who sometimes even smiled and spoke to me were so consumed with hatred for me that one of them might actually kill me just to keep me from registering to vote. If our first small step toward freedom—registering to vote— threatened white folks that much, I knew then that the right to vote must be a powerful thing. And that's the day I realized I was willing to die for the right to vote. I made up my mind: If I ain't got no freedom, I would rather be dead.

All my life I'd known something was wrong with the way I lived. If God was good and loved all his people, as I'd been taught, why did white folks have everything and we got nothing? Didn't the white folks have the same God and read the same Bible? It's strange how you can know something or think you know something and then still really not know it. You know deep inside that most white people think you're not as good as they are, and that some of them, like the enraged men at the courthouse, actually hate you. They hate you just because of the color of your skin. There's no other reason. You've obeyed the law, you've worked their land, you've never done one thing to harm them. Yet you face this smoldering hatred every day, in big ways and small, and you don't understand.

We stayed all day, but I never got inside the courthouse. The clerk let in only two people, and then she didn't tell them whether they passed or not. But what happened outside the courthouse that day was the turning point of my life.

The men with guns eventually sidled away and kept watch from the other side of the courthouse. But the gaze of that white man was burned into my consciousness. For days those cold hateful eyes glared at me. Over and over I saw their festering violence and felt the hate in them. But why? Why were these white people, who had money and power, consumed with hatred for a bunch of poor, pitiful black folks? Did they have to hate us Nobodies to feel like they were Somebodies? What did they think we could do to hurt them? They couldn't have thought we were going to take their jobs and land. Were they afraid they couldn't function if they weren't in control of us? I was afraid of losing my life. But what were they afraid of? I was beginning to figure out that we were onto something bigger than I had ever dreamed.

She titled the book *Barefootin'*, a word that holds great meaning for Unita. "I stayed barefooted most of the time when I was coming up. I didn't have but one pair of shoes, and they were hand-me-downs, so I didn't have much choice in the matter. But I probably would have gone barefooted even if I'd had a closet full of shoes . . . Barefooted I could run faster, climb higher, and dance longer. I was happy and free."

Barefootin' is a metaphor for her approach to life. "To me barefootin' means facing life as it comes, feeling your way along, figuring out things as you go." She didn't have a master plan for her life, but she was open to possibilities that came along. She was eager to learn, however, and she didn't hesitate to jump into things she didn't know how to do. Everyday of her life has been an education, she says, and she built upon what she learned each day to reach for the next new thing. "Barefootin' is about moving forward, following a new path, even though you don't know where it will lead you; tearing down roadblocks, cutting new roads, and never forgetting where you started."

Unita Blackwell had found her purpose. It was as if a switch had been flipped and turned her on. She sprang into action. She made three trips to the courthouse before she was allowed to register. By that time she had become a SNCC field worker with her friend and mentor, Fannie Lou Hamer. She had also helped SNCC organize the Freedom Democratic Party and challenge the state and national Democratic Party officials at the 1964 national convention in Atlantic City. One of the goals SNCC had set for the summer was to empower and train grassroots workers to carry on civil rights work in the state after the national staff had left. Unita Blackwell fulfilled their highest expectations.

Within a space of only three years, 1964-67, Unita was instrumental in increasing the state's black voter registration from 20,000 to nearly 200,000 and getting twenty-two black people elected to public office, including the first black member of the Mississippi House of Representatives. During this same period she spearheaded a successful effort to desegregate the schools in her area, among the first in the state. She set up Freedom Schools, helped hundreds of poor people find housing, food and jobs, and worked to establish the state's first head start program. What happened in three short years because of Unita Blackwell and a few other brave souls is nothing short of phenomenal. Unita Blackwell not only turned her own life around—from field hand to professional organizer and political leader—she was also a significant factor in turning the Mississippi power structure upside down and remaking the social and political framework of the state. Congress and the courts made crucial decisions mandating change. Unita Blackwell, however, was on the front lines fighting the entrenched power structure to ensure that the people in Mississippi, from the grassroots up, changed their ways. In so doing, she endured dozens of arrests for made-up infractions, incarceration in a livestock barn for eleven days, cross burnings and homemade bombs exploding in her front yard, slurs and insults continually directed toward her, ongoing surveillance by the State Sovereignty Commission, and countless other threats, large and small. Unita stood firm and never gave up. Her courage seemed to emanate from an inexhaustible source.

Over the years Unita has been asked about the source of her courage. As she wrote in *Barefootin'*:

> *I don't know whether it was courage I had or not. But if it was courage, then this is what I know about courage: you don't have to think about courage to have it. You don't have to feel courageous to be courageous. You don't sit down and say you're going to be courageous. At the moment of action, you don't see it as a courageous act. Courage is the most hidden thing from your eye or mind until after it's done. There's some inner something that tells you what's right. You know you have to do it to survive as a human being. You have no choice.*

Unita Blackwell had more than courage: she had vision. She had discovered her ability to lead others and get things done, and she dreamed for more. She co-founded Mississippi Action for Community Education (MACE), a human rights organization to teach low-income families in the Mississippi Delta how to help themselves. Still a vital force in the Delta, MACE and its offshoot, Delta Foundation, have created jobs, provided training, and sponsored scores of educational and cultural programs. She was the guiding force in setting up a credit union for local residents who couldn't get loans from the bank. Dorothy Height, director of the National Council of Negro Women, recognized her leadership ability and hired her to carry out an innovative home ownership program for poor people in several states. For about a decade she traveled to and from Washington and throughout the county, working with Housing and Urban Development, community leaders and prospective homeowners to make home ownership possible for many people.

When the housing initiative ended, she turned her attention to the conditions in her hometown. Most of its residents had no indoor plumbing; the town had no sewer system, no streetlights or paved streets, no police or fire protection. Unita set out to find a solution, and she did, incorporate the town and apply for federal grants to fund the services. To do so she had to convince the very white people she had been fighting with to support the black people who were most in need of the services. The town was incorporated in 1976 and Unita served as its mayor for twenty years—first black female mayor in the state. In addition to getting the much-needed services, she gained housing for the elderly and established a wide range of social and economic programs to help the poor and unemployed. She was particularly interested in young people, initiating many educational and cultural opportunities exposing them to possibilities for their future. She served as President of the American Association of Black Mayors.

Unita was active locally, regionally, and nationally in many arenas—social, cultural, economic, and political. She served on several official presidential commissions in Jimmy Carter's administration and informally advised presidents from Lyndon Johnson to Bill Clinton. Invited by Shirley MacLaine to accompany her to tour China and make a film about Chinese women, she toured the country and talked with Chinese people before the U.S. and China had diplomatic relations. Upon her return, she became president of the China-America People's Friendship Society, gave lectures throughout this country, and worked to normalize relations between the two countries. During the 1980s and 90s, she made sixteen or more trips to China, introducing American citizens to the country, and she received and assisted many Chinese dignitaries in Mississippi and in Washington.

In 1982, while she was mayor, she was awarded a fellowship to the University of Massachusetts at Amherst, and at the age of fifty she received a master's degree in regional planning. Several years later, the American Planning Association gave her its Distinguished Leadership Award for an Elected Official. She became a fellow of the Institute of Politics at Harvard. She has received several honorary doctorates and dozens of awards for her work. A leadership institute for young women and a national children and families program are named for her. The MacArthur Foundation honored her work as a human rights activist and community leader by awarding her one of its prestigious fellowships, the so-called "genius grant."

For anyone who questions whether an ordinary citizen can accomplish extraordinary things, no better answer exists than the example of Unita Blackwell. She is amazed at her own life story. "I didn't have any of the qualifications a person is supposed to have to do the things I've done. Sometimes it seems I was snatched up and put in those situations. I'd be sitting in some group feeling inadequate, and someone would ask me what I thought. I'd tell them, and they'd say, 'Oh, that's good.'"

"If I can make it, anybody can," she told me. "I look at young people today who are scuffling trying to make it and don't know what they're going to do with their lives. They are just living from one day to the next. But I have hope for them, because I was a person just like that." She wanted her book to show them that they didn't have to accept things the way they were. She hoped the lessons she had learned along the way would help others make more of their lives.

She credits her hard-working, churchgoing family with teaching her to be strong and showing the way by their own example. As a baby, she "rode" her mother's cotton sack when she went to the field to pick cotton. By age six she was picking cotton herself. The older people, especially the women, taught her to think straight and be responsible, using their own "mother wit," memorable sayings that convey the wisdom of the ages: "Don't lay it on the cow when the milk goes sour"; "If you lie down with dogs, you'll get up with fleas"; and (my favorite) "Wear life like a loose garment."

Her family called her "Little Fast Girl" in appreciation of her quick and curious mind, but in apprehension, too, that her precociousness might cause her problems. Like so many strong black elders who never knew anything but hardship and degradation, Unita's parents and grandparents, aunts and uncles protected her and taught her to believe in herself and cope with the meanness in the world. When a white boy called her names and threatened to "come after her," her mother held her young daughter close, and said, "Don't worry, baby. That's just the way white folks is, White folks don't know anything about you, baby. They just don't know any better." From the influence of both her family and her church, she came to possess a faith in a loving, protective God, in the essential goodness of all human-kind, and in her own worth and dignity.

From an influential teacher, Unita learned that she had an uncommon ability to understand people and ideas and to communicate them effectively. It takes only one good teacher to change the course of a child's life. Unita's was Miss Franklin. Unlike most other teachers who favored lighter skinned students, Miss Franklin paid attention to the dark-skinned Unita. She saw a spark of greatness in her, which she encouraged and nurtured by giving her opportunities to participate in the classroom and to shine as a dynamic speaker for the school. "You can be Somebody," Miss Franklin said. Unita never forgot that.

Unita's spark of greatness lies in her native intelligence and in her understanding of people. Unita understands what other people are thinking and feeling often better than they do. She can intuitively assess a person's attitudes, fears, dreams and hopes in an instant, and her assessments are accurate. Miss Height at NCNW saw this ability and asked Unita to accompany her to high-level meetings and "translate" the feelings and attitudes of the others to her. Give Unita the floor and she knows exactly what to say and how to say it to get her point across, whether she is telling stories to civil rights movement people, giving a formal lecture to Harvard students and professors, or talking directly to a powerful political or business leader.

When she needed legislative assistance to incorporate Mayersville, she went to the Speaker of the House, an old-line white conservative who lived in her county, and explained that it was not appropriate for the Speaker to live in the only county with an unincorporated county seat. "It just doesn't look right," she told him. She received the help she needed. She could also help others understand how to bridge the racial gap to get what they wanted. One local white Mississippi businessman trying to get housing for his town complained to her that the black people who would most benefit from the housing program were against it. She told him that he was talking only to the black people who agreed with him. "That won't get you anywhere," she explained. "It will only harden up the division. You need to talk to the people who are giving you the problem and listen to them . . . Now, wouldn't I look like a nut trying to split up the white folks in my community." He took her suggestion, and soon the project was on track.

Unita hadn't always been so diplomatic. It was impossible in the early days of the civil rights movement when the adversaries were entrenched, immovable, even violent. No amount of talking or maneuvering would have convinced the gun-toting men in the pickup trucks who threatened Unita on the courthouse lawn to accept her rights. Also, she says, "My first years in the movement, I was seething with anger. You have to have some anger to get involved in the movement." But she realized that her anger was bothering her more than it was motivating her and she gradually got her anger under control. She learned when to fight meanness and when to laugh at it, when to stand firm and when to work with the opposition.

I came to find out that one of the most liberating things that can happen to you is to face the opposition calmly, declare your position, and come out feeling good about yourself. We have all name-called each other in anger. Through the years, I had seen that some of the most "radical" people were the ones that sold us out and some of the hard-liners have managed to do good things, after all. I look at results. I want to know what you can do and if I can trust you. Then I can decide how far I'm going with you and where I'm not going. That's the way I think, and I've gotten a lot of work done that way.

You don't have to water down the message; I gave it to people straight, but sometimes just a little at a time. I found out that rushing into a group I'd never met before with ultimatums never works, or not for very long. To work with others to solve problems or to persuade people to consider new ideas and new ways of thinking, you have to listen to people and try to understand where they're coming from,

what their concerns and needs are. And then give them some wiggle
room and time. When you're solving problems and negotiating through
people's differences—whatever they are—everybody needs to feel rec-
ognized: everybody wants to come out looking good.

Unita's creativity is abundant in everything she has done. Not in the
sense of creating art or music, but in solving problems. Facing a new problem, difficulty, or obstacle was not the time to complain. It was a reason to
be imaginative, to find a new way, a better way. If groceries cost too much
for individual families, let the town buy them in bulk and make them
available to the people in the community. If poor people can't qualify for
home loans and if federal rental projects become eyesores and security risks
for the community, Unita reasoned, let's allow responsible poor people to
buy federally subsidized houses and train the owners to maintain them.
Local contractors built the houses, local bankers made the loans, and the
government guaranteed them; Unita worked with community leaders and
homeowners. I visited two of the communities that Unita helped create,
where the original residents or their descendants now own their homes outright: The houses are well-kept, the neighborhoods are as pleasant, stable,
and vibrant as any I've seen anywhere, and the homeowners take pride in
where they live. They would not exist but for Unita Blackwell.

In my early discussions with Unita for her book, I asked her about her family's history. Did her family tell stories about her ancestors? No. She knew
very little about her ancestors. Poor rural black people, like those in her
family, she explained, are a people without a past. "When we came over
from Africa., we were stripped of our history. We didn't even get to keep
our names." And from slavery on, as far as she knew, her family had worked
on plantations; no one had ever done anything remarkable to talk about.
Over the course of our succeeding conversations, however, the outlines of
two compelling stories emerged. The details were sketchy, but the essence
of the stories was clear: both her father and her paternal grandfather had
openly disagreed with the white plantation owners for whom they worked,
and both men suffered irreparably as a result. Her grandfather's boss shot

and killed him on the spot in the Louisiana sugar cane field. Years later her own father questioned the judgment of his white Mississippi boss and provoked his rage; fearing for his safety, Unita's daddy fled from the plantation in the middle of the night and never returned.

Such chilling stories could have made Unita fearful, but they didn't. Instead, like many of the struggles in her own journey, they seemed to have empowered her and made her fearless of the consequences. Her people spoke the truth. Her people stood up for their rights and were willing to risk their lives to gain them. This is a moving legacy to grow up with. But the legacy Unita will leave, not just to her own family but to the world, is truly life-changing. You can find strength and power where you least expect it. You can challenge injustice and win. You can challenge your own limitations and win. You can barefoot your way to a life of meaning and purpose.

Unita Blackwell's name is synonymous with courage and character, vision, determination and faith. A sharecropper's daughter with a sixth-grade education, she overcame staggering odds to become a dynamic civil rights leader, the innovative mayor of her town for twenty years, and a public figure on the national and international stage. Unita Blackwell has dedicated her entire adult life to making our world a more just, more humane place. For nearly fifty years she has been a driving force for change—a legend in her home state of Mississippi, an example of the possibilities of personal growth and fulfillment, the embodiment of civic responsibility and service to others, and a beacon of hope for people everywhere.

You can do it. Your spirit is in your feet, and your spirit can run free.

Betty Pearson

"If one southern family can change this much in my
lifetime, surely, there is hope for the larger society."

*Betty Pearson, 89, a product of a traditional white southern family, witnessed
the overt racism of segregation, the blatant unfairness of the Emmett Till trial
in 1955 which ultimately prompted her to take a leadership role in promot-
ing change by accepting an appointment to the Biracial Mississippi Advisory
Committee to the United States Commission on Civil Rights. She said, "It
absolutely killed my father. He told me it was a betrayal of my heritage."*

I grew up in the Mississippi Delta, "the most southern place on earth" according to James C. Cobb in his book of that name.[1] It is a landscape of broad, fertile fields punctuated with tall cypress trees, a place of haunting beauty to those who love it, and a mosquito-ridden swamp to those who don't. Because of the labor requirements for first clearing the land, and then cultivating it, African-Americans have always been a majority of the population. It is the cradle of the civil rights movement in Mississippi, the place where civil rights leaders Fannie Lou Hamer and Aaron Henry lived and worked, and where Emmett Till was murdered.

My great-grandfather was one of the early white settlers who bought land soon after the Civil War, cleared the cypress trees, the hardwood and the cane brakes, and planted cotton. I grew up on a cotton farm in the 1920's, and although I had black playmates, and felt safe and cared for by the people who worked on the farm and in my grandmother's garden, it never occurred to me as a child to question why I lived in a big white house and they lived in small, unpainted cypress cabins. One of those cabins was just down a dusty path from our house, and the elderly black woman who lived there entertained us for hours with her stories of "slavery time." We were too young to understand the significance of her stories—I thought she was spinning yarns about living in some exotic country far away. In later years I've wondered if the black children who listened with us were as confused as we were, or if they knew they were learning a history that would haunt all of us for the rest of our lives.

In many ways it was an ideal childhood with no television or organized sports, totally unlike anything my grandchildren experienced. We went barefoot all summer, climbed trees and built tree houses, rode our

---

1 Cobb, James C., "The Most Southern Place on Earth," Oxford University Press, June, 1994.

ponies all over the farm, helped feed chickens and pick vegetables. The first Christmas tree I remember had real candles because we had no electricity, and I remember the excitement when we got our first radio (which you could only listen to through earphones).

My paternal grandmother was the most influential person in my life. When I was 18 months old my mother took my grandparents and me for a vacation on the Gulf Coast. Coming home we were struck by a train in the small Delta town of Glendora. I had been sitting on my grandmother's lap in the back seat (long before the days of seat belts or infant car seats!) and the impact tossed me out of the open window and onto the "cowcatcher" of the train that hit us. When the train stopped, I rolled off and was carried back to my mother by a small boy. My grandfather was killed instantly and my grandmother badly injured. The story of the train wreck and my miraculous salvation became my favorite bedtime story, and in telling it my grandmother always ended with "God reached down and plucked you from in front of the train because he has something special he wants you to do with your life."

That story became both a source of pride (after all, none of my friends was ever saved from a speeding train!), and, as I realized only many years later, a burden, because it gave me an exaggerated sense of personal responsibility. During the 1960's I had a gnawing sense of guilt, a feeling that there was something I was supposed to be doing to solve the racial conflict. Now I know that my grandmother's interpretation of the wreck had left me feeling that I had been chosen to be a savior. It has been a great relief to finally realize that my African-American friends were perfectly capable of solving these problems; all they needed from me was my support.

Our house had a wide screen porch across the front where my mother and grandmother and great aunt sat and sewed under ceiling fans while my brother and I played under upturned chairs that we had turned into "forts." One summer day when I was 7 or 8, there was a knock at the back door and my mother told me to go see who was there. I came back and told her that a lady wanted to talk to her. Later she said, "Betty, that

wasn't a lady, that was a Negro woman; only white people are called lady."
The next day when my grandmother and I were in the garden alone, she
told me that although she didn't like to contradict my mother, she needed
to tell me that what my mother had told me wasn't true. My grandmother
said that a person was a lady if she acted like a lady and that being black
or white had nothing to do with it. That made sense to me; I think that
day a seed was planted that grew into my later questioning of segregation
and the idea of racial superiority.

My grandmother also told me stories about the white men who had
Negro mistresses and the white women who knew about their children's
Negro half-brothers and sisters. I think it was the way she told me these
things that influenced me. She didn't tell me that these relationships were
right or wrong, but there was nothing in her stories of the horrors of mis-
cegenation that colored the whispers I overheard from other adults. Even
today I'm not sure what she believed, but she was always so loving and
non-judgmental that the message I received was that all people are equal.

My grandmother also told me the story of her husband's mother, my
great-grandmother. My great-grandfather, one of the early cotton planters
in the Delta, was also a great bear hunter. He had a hunting camp in the
woods and after the crops were harvested he spent weeks at a time there
taking servants, wagon loads of food and a pack of bear dogs. It is difficult
to imagine today what a hardship this was for his wife. She was left at the
farm, with servants to be sure, but with no other companionship for weeks
on end. There were no paved or even gravel roads and during the winter
months the dirt roads were almost impassable. Sometime around 1890
the railroad between New Orleans and Memphis was being built and, for
the next several years, the advance man for the Illinois Central RR stayed
at my great-grandfather's home when he was in the Delta making deals for
the right-of-way. So he was there sometime in the 1890s when the man of
the house was away on a hunting trip. When my great-grandfather and his
two teen-aged sons returned, he found that his wife had run off to South
America with "Mr. Norton."

The sequel to this story says a lot about my grandmother's character.
Around 1910, after my grandmother and grandfather had married and

had a son (my father), they received a phone call from New Orleans. It was my great-grandmother calling to say that Mr. Norton had died in South America and, that learning she had cancer, she wanted to come home to die. My grandfather, still feeling the anger of having been abandoned, wanted to say "no," but my grandmother's response was that "this is your mother. Of course we will take her in and care for her." In my living room today I have the trunk she took to South America and brought back with her, and so my daughter, my granddaughter and I stand in a line of feminists going back more than a hundred years!

Perhaps it was these stories my grandmother told me, "the myths of my childhood," that made me always feel a little different. During the 1960s, for example, it didn't take any great courage to stand against the status quo. It was much more a question of "Who am I and what must I do?"

The other person who influenced me was my father. He was a strong man, very much the extrovert, a leader who genuinely liked people. He taught us to ride and to hunt and he encouraged independence of spirit. He was as honest a man as I've ever known; he taught my brother and me to be responsible for our own behavior and to always do what we knew was right, no matter what our peers thought—a lesson that back-fired in the 1960s when what I thought was right differed so much from his own values. I adored him; the most painful thing for me during the civil rights days was that, in standing against segregation, I was standing against my father. Following his death, it was a great comfort when Aaron Henry called and said, "Betty, your father was a good man. His office was one of the few in Clarksdale I could enter knowing I would be treated with respect. I know that you disagree with him about race, but just remember that he was the product of his upbringing." I found that willingness to understand and forgive in many of the black leaders of the movement.

My father's "upbringing" meant that he was good to the black people who worked for him, but it was always a paternalistic relationship. He took care of them in the same way he took care of his children. Underneath was the firmly held belief that black people were innately inferior to whites.

All of the schools I attended, including college, were of course segregated. As I grew older I no longer had black friends my age, although we always had a black cook, a black gardener and a black man who drove my grandmother. An interesting tidbit about the segregated schools at that time is the different meaning given to "colored" in different Delta towns. In Clarksdale, the Chinese children were sent to the black schools, while in Sumner they went to the white schools.

By the time I went off to college in the fall of 1940 I was sure in my belief that a segregated society was wrong and that people were just people, regardless of skin color. Fortunately, I found a few people at Ole-Miss who agreed with me, including my roommate, Florence Mars. When World War II started the University of Mississippi went to a year-round schedule; Florence and I decided to go to summer school for two summers and graduate early. Those summers were unbelievably hot and there was no air conditioning in dorms or classrooms. One torrid day when I went to the college laundry to pick up some clothes, I bemoaned the heat to the (black) laundry worker. She said, "If you think this is hot you should go to the back of this laundry. There are no fans, we are sweltering and we don't make enough to suffer like this." More to make conversation than as a deliberate act of provocation, I replied "You should go on strike. With this heat, and the campus full of students, the University can't afford to let the laundry shut down." Several days later she found me in my room and told me the workers had decided to strike and they wanted me to go with them as their representative to talk to the Chancellor and the laundry manager. I wasn't at all keen on this proposal, but since I had started it I felt I had no choice. I talked Florence into going with me, and our efforts were successful in getting the laundry workers a small pay raise, better hours and the addition of some large fans. Chancellor Butts, who was a college friend of my father, called him and told him that if I did any more labor agitating on campus I would be expelled. That night I got a call from a very angry parent.

Another influence during my college years was majoring in philosophy. Studying ethics, reading the history of philosophers who had struggled with the meaning of good and evil, the long discussions in our class about what it meant to lead a good life, all served to clarify my values.

My senior year in college I was awarded a scholarship for graduate work at Columbia University. I was ecstatic, but my father was adamant in his opposition to my accepting the offer. He had the prevalent southern distrust of the big city, particularly the northern big city and he couldn't imagine his only daughter being alone in New York for two years. I was too young and still too attached to home and family to defy him, so I turned the scholarship down. However, it made me so angry and unsure of what I wanted to do with my life that the week after graduation I drove to Memphis and enlisted in the Marine Corps. After boot camp and officer training in North Carolina, I was commissioned a second lieutenant and spent the rest of World War II at bases in California. Joining the Marine Corps was perhaps the best thing I've ever done for myself. It gave me the opportunity to get away from Mississippi and my family and to grow up a little. I had led an isolated and protected life and, for the first time, I was truly on my own. I met and made friends with people from all over the country, many from backgrounds and with views radically different from mine. I think being a Marine gave me the courage to stand up against my parents and most of the white society in Mississippi during the 50's and 60's.

When the war was over, I thought about staying in California and getting an advanced degree through the GI Bill of Rights. However, because I had no clear idea of what I wanted to do, I returned to Mississippi to visit my family and old friends. At about same time my future husband, Bill Pearson, came back to Mississippi after service in the Army Air Corps. His uncle had died suddenly, and Bill was asked by his family to come home and manage Rainbow Plantation, the family farm of approximately 2500 acres, near Webb, Mississippi and about 25 miles from my home in Clarksdale. Bill and I had never dated or gone to the same schools, but our parents were friends. I had gone to camp with his sister and we had gone to the same parties and dances since we were 13 or 14 years old. In 1945, with the war over, we renewed our acquaintance with each other and with our high school and college friends, many of them now married and starting families. It was a wonderful summer of days at Moon Lake, picnics on sand bars in the Mississippi River and dinners with friends.

We were married in February, 1947 and moved to Rainbow Plantation, where we lived until 1994, when Bill retired and sold the land. I loved living in the country and became an ardent gardener, but the injustices of both the plantation system and the segregated society as a whole became increasingly more apparent and immediate to both of us. For example, our daughter went to a two-story brick school in the nearby town of Sumner, while the children of our workers were crowded into a one-room "school" in the black Baptist church on the farm. Every element of society was segregated: schools, restaurants, public restrooms, doctors' offices, even water fountains, and we soon learned that we were in the very small minority of the white population who believed that segregation should end and that this country should become a truly open, equal and free society. We were able to gradually improve living conditions for our workers, but it was much more difficult to change the culture of paternalism, not to mention the seeming impossibility of ever changing the segregated society in which we all lived. Bill wanted his workers to be more independent and to accept responsibility for their own lives, but it was an uphill battle, because it was everyone's expectation, black and white, that the plantation owner "took care" of his people. In spite of our efforts it took twenty years, and the civil rights movement, before there was much change in those attitudes.

In 1955 Emmett Till, a 14 year old black youth from Chicago who had been visiting family was murdered for allegedly making a pass at a white woman; the trial was set for Sumner (because it was believed that the murder took place in Tallahatchie County, which later proved not to be the case). When J. W. Milam and Roy Bryant, half-brothers, were indicted for kidnapping Emmet Till, they first came to Harvey Henderson, a lawyer in Sumner and Bill's childhood friend, who had been best man in our wedding. Harvey told them that he only accepted civil cases, not trial work, and referred them to his law partner, Sidney Carlton. It infuriated me that all of the lawyers in West Tallahatchie County, including Harvey and another close friend, Johnny Whitten, banded together to be the defense team for Milam and Bryant. J. W. Kellen was a member of the defense team whom I knew only casually. He was originally from Tutwiler and did not go to law school, but passed the Bar by "reading" with an older lawyer. John Whitten practiced law in Sumner. He was a first cousin of Jamie Whitten, long time U.S. Representative from Charleston.

I understood that under our legal system everyone is entitled to legal representation, but for every lawyer in the area to be part of the defense team indicated to the country and to the world that all of the white people in Mississippi were defending the murderers, and I knew that wasn't true. At that time I had never attended a trial of any kind (in 1955 white women could vote but were not called for jury duty) but I decided to go to this trial to see for myself what happened and through Bill's uncle, who owned the local newspaper, I secured two press passes. Florence Mars, my college roommate and life-long friend, came up and together we sat through the five days of the trial.

On the first day, as we were about to enter the back door to the courthouse, which was the entrance for the press, the ex-sheriff stopped me and said, "Betty, you shouldn't be going to this trial." When I asked him why he said, "You will be hearing things that no white lady should hear." I thanked him for his concern and went on into the courthouse. The trial was an eye-opener for me. I had grown up in a segregated society and understood how racist it was, but my experience had been of a very paternalistic racism, misguided but never violent. Looking at the faces of the white people in that courtroom made me realize how deep and mean the feelings actually were. I saw pure hatred. The courtroom was packed. They had brought in cane chairs for the overflow. There were men sitting in the open windows. Most of the audience was white and friends of the defendants. In the very back of the room there was a row of black people standing up. There was one table for black reporters just outside the rail that separated onlookers from active participants. Inside the rail were two tables for the white press. Except for the court stenographer, Florence and I were the only women inside the rail.

September is always one of the hottest months in the Delta, and that year was no exception. There were four ceiling fans stirring the air, but it was still like sitting in an oven. When I saw the expressions on the faces of the men in the jury I whispered to Flossie, "They'll never convict." But as the trial went on it became clear that, even with an impartial jury, it would have been hard to get a conviction, because the sheriff testified for the defense rather than for the prosecution and refused to identify the body or give a cause of death.

On the second day the prosecution asked for a recess because they had learned of two new witnesses and wanted to call them. The judge granted the recess, but the witnesses could not be found. The buzz among the press corps was that the sheriff had sequestered, in the jail in Charleston, two young black men who had been witnesses to the murder and then told the prosecuting attorneys that they were not, in fact, in his jail. The most dramatic testimony came from Mose Wright when he identified Milam and Bryant as the two men who had come to his house and taken Emmett away. It is hard to imagine today how courageous it was in 1955 for an elderly black man to make that kind of accusation. I didn't know Mose Wright, I understood he was a highly respected member of the black community in LeFlore County (he was a farmer near Money, the site of the Bryant's Store and Till's encounter with Mrs. Bryant, which is close to Greenwood, the county seat). After the trial, I don't know whether or not he was actually threatened, but in several instances, men drove by his house shooting guns. Mose Wright and his wife, Sue, left Mississippi and moved to Chicago. There was little trust or understanding between the races and most black people were afraid, stayed at home during the trial and were reluctant to even talk about it to a white person either at the time or much later. I think the Emmett Till murder, and especially his mother's courage in showing the world what had happened to her son, was the catalyst for the civil rights movement. It was to be another nine or ten years before any real change took place.

The Till trial also threw into sharp relief, for me at least, the unspoken and largely unacknowledged class structure of society in the Delta. Apart from the sharp divide between blacks and whites, there were in the white community, two classes: the land-owners and professionals who belonged to the country clubs, attended the same parties and sent their children to the same colleges, in contrast to poorer whites, who hadn't been to college, did not own land and worked for hourly wages. It was unacknowledged because it challenged our belief in America as a classless society, but it was true nonetheless. Thus, when being interviewed for this book and asked what standing Mr. Bryant and Mr. Milam had in the community, the only honest answer was "I have no idea." I had never met either man or even heard of them. During the trial the people I knew, although annoyed because they could hardly get to the post office or grocery store, due to the crowds, stayed away from the courthouse, didn't talk about the trial and were a bit scandalized that Florence and I attended. On the other hand, the families and friends of Milam and Bryant filled the courtroom every day with an overflow to the benches outside.

In the months following the trial, Mr. Bryant's store was boycotted, first by blacks, but later by the very people who had been supportive during the trial. When the two men sold the story of their guilt in the kidnapping and murder to LOOK magazine, these people felt betrayed and it was their anger and animosity which finally drove the two men to leave the state.

In 1959 or 1960 the Bishops of the Catholic, Episcopal and Methodist churches formed the Mississippi Council on Human Relations and both Florence and I were asked to be board members. The Citizens Council had already been founded based on wide-spread opposition to the integration of public schools. The Human Relations Council was a totally integrated group which started with the idea of the importance of furthering communication between the races and of having a leadership forum to hear about and deal with problems as they arose. It was at these meetings that I came to know and admire the courage of some of the black leaders like Aaron Henry, Fannie Lou Hamer and Amzie Moore. It was here, too, that Florence and I finally met other white Mississippians who felt as we did. I had felt very isolated in my small part of the Delta and it was good to know that there were other white people, scattered across the state, who would join me in fighting for an integrated society.

It was at a human relations conference at Tougaloo College that I was asked if I would accept an appointment to the Mississippi Advisory Committee to the United States Civil Rights Commission. Ideally, from a state like Mississippi, the Committee would be bi-racial, and although there was not a problem in finding black leaders to serve, finding whites was another matter. I accepted the appointment which initiated the break-down of my relationship with my parents; it was very painful to me, and I'm sure to them as well. A few days after my appointment, there was an article in the Memphis Commercial Appeal announcing the names of the members of the Mississippi Committee. My father arrived at our door that morning, newspaper in hand literally in tears. He begged me not to serve on this integrated committee, which he said would make me "a trai-tor to your people and your heritage."

I loved my parents, especially my father, and I did not want to hurt him, but in this case I could see no choice. If I was to live with myself for the rest of my life, I had to be true to what I knew was right. I said, "But Dad, all my life you've taught me to do what I know is right, re-gardless of the consequences or the opinions of others." I think that it had never occurred to him that my idea of what was right would ever be different from his. Thus began what was the most painful period of my life. I do not compare my experience with that of the true heroines of the civil rights movement, those brave black women who were arrested and beaten time after time, only to come back and try once more to register to vote. I never felt in any physical danger, but the emotional stress of my parents' unhappiness and the disapproval of many of my old friends was hurtful and constant. I tried to maintain a quasi-normal relationship with my parents for the sake of our daughter, their first grandchild, whom they adored, but it wasn't easy at best, and sometimes was very painful. It was never more than an armed truce.

Brown vs. Board of Education was decided in 1954, but 10 years later few moves had been made to integrate Mississippi schools. However, the Justice Department had begun to initiate cases and so sometime in the mid 1960s, when our Committee was slated to go to Washington to meet with the Civil Rights Commission, the attorney for the local school board called me and asked me to talk to anyone in Washington who could give me information that would be helpful to the school board. I took the assignment seriously and talked to many people, especially in the Justice Department. When I got home I called the attorney and told him I had what I felt was good news. The people to whom I had talked understood the problems involved in integrating schools in a county like ours, where there was a large majority of black students and where the public schools had been so unequal in the past. What they wanted was *intent* to integrate and if we came up with a reasonable plan, they would give us the years we would need to implement it. I suggested that we could, integrate the first grade each year and in twelve years the schools would be integrated. To my astonishment, his response was that he wasn't even going to tell the school board what I had reported. He said that they would never integrate the schools and that he had hoped I could tell them some way to avoid this process. I told him that in that case, instead of doing it gradually and on their own terms, the schools would be integrated suddenly, by court order, which was of course what eventually happened. This is just one example of the emotional and completely unreasonable attitude of so many of the white "leaders."

I had met Aaron Henry at the Human Relations Council meetings. It was sometime in the mid-sixties that I drove to Clarksdale to talk to him and subsequently became a card-carrying member of the NAACP. I had realized by then that my role in the civil rights movement would be largely symbolic—showing that there were white people whose families had been here for generations but who were ardently opposed to a segregated society. I would actively and openly support the people on the front lines, both Mississipians and civil rights workers, who came into the state, the "outsiders," who were being blamed for all of our racial problems. Bill and I encouraged the people who worked on our farm to register to vote and I went to the courthouse with the first few to get that process started.

Through my participation on the Advisory Committee, I met many of the young lawyers and students who were in Mississippi doing civil rights work during those years. Living on a plantation in the country was a great boon because we were secluded and no one could watch who came and went. Rainbow became a kind of safe place where they could unwind, rest, have sympathetic company and good food.

That led to another unpleasant incident with my family. I didn't try to force on them any of the students, who were sometimes a bit scruffy, but one couple we became friendly with (and who have become life-long friends) I thought no one could possibly raise objections.

John "Jack" Doyle was a young New York lawyer who had taken a leave of absence from his firm to work with what was called "The President's Committee." He had been sent to Mississippi by the American Bar Association at the request of President Lyndon Johnson. He was a very proper, well-mannered young man, always dressed in coat and tie. His wife, Mary Ellen, was an artist, and when I learned they weren't going home for Christmas, I invited them to spend Christmas with us. Our Christmas tradition in those years was a big family dinner at my parents' home on Christmas Eve and Christmas day dinner at Rainbow, with both my parents and Bill's. Everything went well, and I thought that, at least, we had shown them that civil rights workers could be nice people, but that was not to be. Nothing was said at the time, but evidently feelings smoldered.

When Ole Miss played a football game in Jackson the following fall, we invited Mary Ellen and Jack to go with us, not so much for the game as for the tailgate picnic which we thought they would enjoy. My father was a rabid Ole Miss fan; for the games in Jackson he had a suite at a local motel and a big spread of food and drinks after each game. After the game we went there, chatted, introduced Mary Ellen and Jack to the other guests and left thinking everything was fine. Three days later I received a letter (typed by his secretary) from my father informing me that Bill and I were always welcome, but that he didn't want any more civil rights workers brought to his home or to any party he was giving. I was stunned and hurt and furious that he couldn't even talk to me about it, but had to send an impersonal letter. Needless to say, that was the last time we went to any of their parties.

In 1968, Bill was a member of the bi-racial delegation to the Democratic Convention in Chicago that successfully challenged the "regular" white delegation. It was a huge political victory after the unsuccessful attempt by Fannie Lou Hamer and others, at the 1964 convention, to represent the people of Mississippi that led to the flight of most white Mississippians to the Republican party. Bill's participation also offended our families and many of our old friends.

In 1969, the year after Martin Luther King was assassinated, there was a memorial march in Memphis and I participated with two friends (the marchers were probably 4 to 1 black to white). We marched from a church in south Memphis all the way up Main Street to City Hall and, although the march was entirely peaceful, there were armed National Guardsmen every few feet down each side of the street. It was an eerie feeling, at least to me, to be walking down a street in this country with such a strong armed presence. It gave me new insight into how threatened black people have always felt, in ways that whites have never realized.

During the 60s we had numerous nasty phone calls, lost a white carpenter who had done a lot of work on our house because his wife didn't want him to work for n----- lovers, had problems with some of the members of our church who objected to workshops for volunteer reading teachers at the penitentiary because black volunteers were included, and in general, became "outsiders" in the society in which we had grown up.

In 1972, our daughter, Erie, who had graduated from Swarthmore College, married Michael Vitiello, a boy from New Jersey, whom she had met in college. Erie had always wanted to be married at home so we planned a garden wedding at Rainbow. My parents weren't sure about their granddaughter marrying a Yankee, but they rallied and said that they, with my brother and his wife, would host the rehearsal dinner the night before the wedding. Then Erie told us that Michael's sister was married to a black man. When we told my parents, they were stunned and said they couldn't possibly have the rehearsal dinner because of "what people would think." If we went on with a home wedding, where would this couple stay? I said, "With us, of course," and told them that while they were welcome to be a part of the celebration, all of Michael's family would be there and were welcome. Andy and Oscar Carr and their wives, old friends from Clarksdale, hosted the rehearsal dinner in Susie and Andy's home, and other friends, Jane and Wes Watkins from Greenville, had a dinner party the night before. The wedding was a smashing success. Many of Erie and Mike's college friends came down for a week of parties, picnics and softball games. Our close friends, while perhaps not agreeing with us about mixed marriages, were constant in their love, and put on a wonderful wedding luncheon for 200 or so guests.

My parents attended the wedding. At one point in the afternoon, I saw my father in conversation with Erie's black brother-in-law. When they left, I walked them to their car and told my father how glad I was they had come. I said "I know this hasn't been easy for you and that you're here because you love Eric and me. Thanks for being nice to Mel." Tears rolled down his cheeks.

This uneasy relationship with my parents culminated in the reading of my mother's will in which she did not leave me the land she had always promised. My father explained that she was afraid that if she left it to me a black person would eventually own it. That kind of paranoia is difficult to understand and the feeling of rejection remains.

When our grandchildren were born we decided to put in a swimming pool. Both of them learned to swim there. Since there were no swimming pools in the area that were open to black children, I decided to have swimming lessons for all of the children on the farm. White children learned to swim at private clubs or summer camps, but there was no swimming instruction for black children and many of them grew up unable to swim and afraid of the water. For the ten years that we had the pool before Bill retired and we sold the land, we had swimming lessons two afternoons a week for all of the children who lived on Rainbow and later for any children related to the families who lived there. I got a lot of personal satisfaction from the fact that every child on the place, with the exception of my housekeeper's grandson (whom I could never coax off the steps), learned to swim and eventually dived (or jumped) off the board. At the end of each summer we had a party for the parents and grandparents so they could see what the children had learned.

Now in my 87th year I feel as if I've come full circle from the week in 1955 when I sat through the Till trial. I was thirty-three years old at the time, and thought that certainly by the turn of a new century, I would be living in a peacefully integrated society. Perhaps I am naive, but I still have hope. The Tallahatchie County Board of Supervisors has appointed a bi-racial Emmett Till Memorial Commission for the purpose of "fostering racial harmony and reconciliation, to seek funds to restore the courthouse in Sumner (to 1955), establish an Emmett Till Museum and promote educational tours of the courthouse and other historical sites." I am co-chairman of the commission, along with Mayor Robert Grayson of Tutwiler, who grew up on our farm and whose little brother was one of our daughter's playmates. For the first time in the sixty years that I have lived here blacks and whites have entered into an open and honest discussion of our problems and the possible solutions. There are still disagreements and sometimes expressions of distrust, but we discuss issues openly now, which gives me hope that real change is still possible. There has been a great deal of progress since the 1950s, but we still have a long way to go. Restaurants are integrated, but schools and churches are not. There is very little bi-racial socializing, and this is in large measure due to the great difference in educational opportunities.

My primary hope, however, lies with future generations. My grandchildren are truly color-blind. They have an African-American uncle and first cousins whom they adore. The society I grew up in would be as foreign to them as "slavery times" was to me. On the other side of our family, my husband's great-niece married a black man last spring in a wedding that was a joyous and loving celebration of different colors, accents and ideas. We are looking forward to welcoming a new little "great-great" next spring. If one Southern family can change this much in my lifetime, surely, there is hope for the larger society.

Florence Mars

"Witness in Philadelphia, Mississippi—
A Civil Rights Champion"
"What a witness! She witnessed with her eyes,
her ears and her heart. She saw, she heard, she felt
and through her own involvement she bore witness
to qualities of courage and good will that all but
evaporated in the climate of passion that flowed
from an unreasoning fear of change."

—Turner Catledge, Executive Editor, New York Times

Stanley Dearman

Stanley Dearman is retired editor and publisher of the Neshoba Democrat, a newspaper in Philadelphia, Mississippi for which he worked for 40 years until 2000. He was awarded the University of Mississippi's most prestigious journalism award, the Silver Em Award, which recognizes an outstanding journalist with a Mississippi connection. Dearman had been editor of the Campus newspaper at the University of Mississippi during his senior year in 1959. He was inducted into the Mississippi Press Association's Hall of Fame in June, 2005. He was the first recipient in 1989 of the Neshoba County's Citizen of the Year Award. Dearman took over operation of the Neshoba Democrat at a time when the county had become infamous for the disappearance of three young men during the 1964 "Freedom Summer" campaign. Stan Dearman was a lifelong friend of Florence Mars.

Florence Latimer Mars was born on January 1, 1923 to Adam Longino Mars, a lawyer, and Emily Geneva Johnson Mars, known as Neva. Both their families were early settlers when Neshoba County was created in 1833 from Choctaw Indian Land. She was born in the large Victorian home of her grandfather, Dr. William Henry Mars, on Holland Avenue in Philadelphia, Mississippi. Dr. Mars, who performed the delivery, no longer practiced medicine, but as a matter of pride, wanted to deliver his own grandchild, according to Florence's maternal aunt, Ellen Johnson Spendrup. It was a difficult delivery and Florence suffered some permanent effects from it. One leg was shorter than the other and she walked with a slight limp all her life.

A large part of Florence's childhood was spent riding around the county with her grandfather, Dr. Mars (whom she called Poppaw), to inspect his property, which consisted of 17,000 acres of land in Neshoba County. The property also included tenant housing for both black and white families. One of these houses, in the old Mars homestead east of Philadelphia, was occupied by a black family. As Florence wrote: "Aunt Min Ross very often cooked up something out of deference for Poppaw's large appetite. As we sat in a warm cozy kitchen and joined the laughter and good humor, I began to contrast the circumstances with the attitudes of his white tenants. The gracious ways of Negro tenants, the sense of humor in the face of their adversities was impressive and set me on a course of wondering why. At an early age I concluded that it was faith in God and the promise of a heavenly reward that was responsible for their good humor and patience."

Florence began to notice other things, including the variation in the color of some Negroes. She began to learn which white families were related to them as a result of "night time integration."

Florence described in her book *Witness in Philadelphia* (1977) the conversations that occurred at the dining room table at her home in Philadelphia: "The habit of conversation was a long time tradition in Poppaw's house. I listened to the table talk between my father and his father. More often, the discussion involved a legal question or politics. I began to want to take part . . . but my mother disapproved. She looked on the heated discussions as arguments and wasn't pleased when I tried to take part. The men indulged me anyway, up to a certain point."

Florence began forming strong opinions the more she thought about the things she observed again from her book: "The Christian teachings of brotherhood and sending missionaries to Africa to save lost souls began to disgust me, but I tried to cover that up too. One day, while we were sitting on a boat, I tried to talk to Daddy's brother, Jim, about the church's attitude toward White Supremacy, but he was noncommittal. Perhaps he was afraid of disturbing my views. It wasn't just the hard physical activity that was distressing me about the separate life of the Negro—white people worked hard also—it was the way they were treated." Even to suggest that the degrading use of the "For Colored Only" signs was not right, brought nothing but disapproval, Florence noted.

It was these early childhood observations and other significant events that impacted Florence's life and led to her challenging the *status quo* in working to help the plight of the Negro in the South. One such event occurred 11 years before the celebrated civil rights case involving the deaths of Michael Schwerner, Andrew Goodman and James Chaney, civil rights activists killed by the Klu Klux Klan in Philadelphia, Mississippi in 1964. This was the case of the last will and testament of Sim Burnside that occurred in 1953. The injustice of breaking the will in favor of white cousins in this mixed racial family disturbed Florence Mars because it represented racial discrimination against the people involved. Florence said, "The lifelong tensions I had felt over the race issue began to increase." Despite Burnside's will having been drawn up by an attorney and having each page signed and witnessed by the deputy chancery clerk and county supervisor, the will was overturned on the testimony of a number of people who declared that Sim Burnside, at age 82, was "not in his right mind." Sim Burnside, the last survivor of a large family, left the entire estate to the people of Neshoba County to be used as a game refuge with a lake for fishing. Signs were to be placed throughout the park designating it as the Burnside Memorial Park.

The Burnside family's story was legendary, passed down from generation to generation. It began after Indian land was opened up for settlement after the Treaty of Dancing Rabbit Creek in 1830. William Alexander Burnside came from South Carolina in 1850 with his slaves and began fathering children by one of them, a light-skinned Mulatto named Mariah, when she was 17 and he was 40. When the slaves were freed, there were five children; three more were born later. Unlike other night time integrations, Burnside made this former slave his common law wife and heir, along with the children, over the protest of his parents and two brothers, who also came into Neshoba from South Carolina. As Florence wrote in her book, *The Bell Returns to Mount Zion,* in 1996: "A powerful and influential man in the early history of this sparsely settled rural land, W. A. Burnside saw to it that his wife and children lived the life of white people. However, admitting the circumstances of their birth to themselves, the offspring made a pact (among themselves) never to marry."

The family lived out their lives in one household. W.A. Burnside died in 1891 and Mariah lived until 1925. As the children died, there was no need to divide the estate.

At Sim Burnside's death on December 31, 1952, the estate consisted of large holdings of money and land. The white Burnsides, now down to second cousins, were quick to file suit for the money and the land as soon as the law would allow. The fast moving trial went to a jury on the fourth day at 11:00 p.m. Numerous witnesses were called who claimed that Sim Burnside was not in his right mind. One hour and 10 minutes later, the jury of all white males returned a verdict in favor of the white cousins. The verdict was upheld in an appeal to the Mississippi Supreme Court. Lawyers who fought to break the will had signed contracts for half the proceeds. Florence Mars was very disturbed by this and said, "All my life I had watched juries give verdicts based on the biases of those who made the decisions, but denying this family's right to honor the life they were forced to live was the most tragic I had known about up to that time."

Florence continued to feel outrage at the injustice of the result of the

Burnside case. When she wrote about it in 1996, she had her lawyer requisition the case file from the archives of the Mississippi Supreme Court and studied it in detail. It was rather like opening an old wound. Florence did receive a measure of satisfaction, however, despite the verdict in the case, because of the way in which Federal funds were approved for a park project supporting Burnside Lake and a portion of the original land. Burnside Park opened for recreation and included the lake for fishing. Florence Mars notes in her book: "Burnside Lake Park exists with more facilities than . . . the Burnside family could have ever imagined. . . . The park is going well, enjoyed by all races, colors and creeds, and has become irrevocably linked in my mind with a Twenty Five Year Commemoration honoring those the Ku Klux Klan murdered." Florence saw the final result of the project akin to poetic justice.

A graduate of Philadelphia High School, Florence attended Millsaps College in Jackson, Mississippi. She transferred to the University of Mississippi and graduated in 1944. Afterwards, she worked for Delta Airline in Atlanta as a reservations agent. In the 1950s, she lived in New Orleans and photographed jazz musicians. She returned to Philadelphia in 1962 to raise cattle and own and operate the Neshoba County Stockyards.

This very private woman might have continued to live the quiet life she preferred had it not been for her shock and outrage when three young civil rights workers were murdered by the White Knights of the Klu Klux Klan near her hometown, Philadelphia, Mississippi on Sunday, June 21, 1964. Her very vocal call for justice ran afoul of the Klan's effort to control what people said and thought and she paid a price for the stand she took.

Florence, who was arrested and jailed for her outspoken resistance to the Klan, credited them with making her better understand the plight of Negroes during the civil rights years. As she explained in her privately published book, *The Bell Returns to Mount Zion*. She met four Negroes while in jail and learned from them about their circumstances. "Among other things, the KKK, in control of the thought patterns of the community, made it possible for me to know four Negroes in a way not previously open to me. . . . We shared some experiences that gave me additional insight into what it had been like to be a Negro at the mercy of the white men's (and women's) whims. . . . These four Negroes, whose roots, like mine, were in the soil of this sparsely populated rural county, were Junior Roosevelt Cole (always called Bud), his wife, Beatrice Clemons Cole, Lillie Calloway Jones, and Clinton Collier. They accepted me, allowed me to identify with them and vice-versa, something I could neither say my mother's bridge club did nor most of the members of the First Methodist Church."

Florence's first book, *Witness in Philadelphia,* published in 1977 by the Louisiana State University Press, describes the murders of the three martyrs, Goodman, Schwerner and Chaney, and the effect it had on her home town. Turner Catledge, who grew up in Philadelphia, Mississippi as a contemporary of Florence's mother, Neva, was executive editor of the New York Times. In the foreword to *Witness in Philadelphia,* he wrote of Florence, "What a witness! She witnessed with her eyes, her ears and her heart. She saw, she heard, she felt and through her own involvement she bore witness to qualities of courage and goodwill that all but evaporated in the climate of passion that flowed from an unreasoning fear of change."

On the night of June 16, five days before the murders, Klansmen, including a group from Meridian, Mississippi, paid a visit to the Mount Zion Methodist Church, a black institution 11 miles east of Philadelphia during a meeting of the Board of Stewards. As members left the building, they were confronted by Klansmen and accused of holding a voter registration school in the church. They were also looking for Michael Schwerner, the white man from New York who had been agitating and encouraging blacks to register to vote. Two men and a woman were beaten. One man, J.R. "Bud" Cole, was beaten so severely that he suffered permanent injuries and was in physical pain the rest of his life. Later that night, the church was burned by the Klan.

Michael Schwerner happened to have been in Oxford, Ohio at a training camp for volunteers, most of them college students, to work in the voter registration project in the South. He returned to Meridian the following Saturday, bringing with him Andrew Goodman. Schwerner and Goodman were white New Yorkers. On Sunday morning, Schwerner and Goodman along with James Chaney, an African American, drove to Neshoba County to investigate the church burning and the beatings.

It was never determined how local law enforcement officers knew the civil rights workers were in the Longdale community that day or a description of the vehicle they were driving. They were stopped later that afternoon on the outskirts of Philadelphia on a trumped up traffic charge. They were taken to jail and held until Klansmen from Philadelphia and Meridian could mobilize. After releasing them around 10:00 p.m., that night, Deputy Sheriff Cecil Price told them to get out of Neshoba County. Several carloads of Klansmen were waiting along the road to intercept their vehicle and take them to a designated spot where they were shot. Their bodies were buried in a farm pond dam seven miles southwest of Philadelphia.

Early the next day agents of the Federal Bureau of Investigation poured into Neshoba County to begin their investigation. Within six weeks, the FBI had located the bodies and knew who was involved. Florence later wrote, "When the murders occurred I was 41 years old, a white, Anglo-Saxon Protestant teaching two classes at the church I attended. Believing that what happens is the sum total of what has gone before and that it applied to me, I could not stand idly by now. I sided with the federal government's aim to solve the crime and began talking openly with members of the FBI. I also testified before an early grand jury hearing about Negroes being beaten by law enforcement officers, something I said I learned from my maid, whom I believed. Other whites were testifying that the Negroes were not telling the truth about their treatment." Almost immediately, she said a concerted propaganda campaign began against her. "I returned from the grand jury hearing on the Mississippi Gulf Coast on a Thursday night. The next day, Friday, members of the Ku Klux Klan were out in force at the Neshoba County Stockyards, which I owned, to say that I was against 'our boys.'"

The Klan organized a boycott against the stockyard where she sold cattle, forcing it to close, and she was made to resign from posts at the

First United Methodist Church. There was a lot of animosity toward her for being so outspoken. She had threats against her life, anonymous midnight phone calls, people driving by her house throwing bricks and shouting obscenities. But she never wavered from her convictions.

Discussing Florence Mars' resistance to the Klan must also include her maternal aunt, Ellen Johnson Spendrup, her mother Neva's older sister. Tough and plainspoken, afraid of nothing, Ellen stood with Florence through the whole ordeal. They thought alike and reached the same conclusions about what was happening. Ellen and Neva, although sisters, were very different. Neva, while progressive in her ideas, was the genteel Southern lady, careful not to offend anyone or ruffle anyone's feathers. Ellen enjoyed ruffling feathers. It didn't matter whose. Ellen loved her late afternoon libations of Bourbon and good conversation. "She could drink you and me both under the table and never show it," Florence told me once. "During one of these occasions I told her she reminded me of Alice Roosevelt Longwood, but with a nicer sense of humor." Ellen said, "I used to see her when I worked in Washington. Her chauffeur used to park her big long black car across the street from my apartment where she frequently visited a friend."

Ellen lived and worked in New Orleans in the 1920s. She met and married a Swedish sea captain, Alex Spendrup, and lived in Gothenburg, Sweden, from 1930 to 1940. She decided to return to the United States when the clouds of war began gathering over Europe. En route to Genoa to board a ship for America, she had a layover of several days in Berlin. One day on a Berlin street, she saw something that was forever etched in her memory: "I saw a line of terribly sad and miserable looking people being marched along to where I don't know. This chain of humanity seemed endless. It went on for blocks and blocks. What I remember so vividly was their pained expression and their meager possessions, in bags and back packs. Some of them had just remnants of shoes on their feet. Some feet were wrapped and tied with whatever material was available. I never learned any details of who they were or where they were going." After the war, however, when a lot of information became known, Ellen had an idea of what it was all about.

Florence wrote of her Aunt Ellen during the civil rights crisis: "Shortly after the disappearance (of the three men) I discovered a hand full of others who also thought that a crime had been committed. My mother, though hesitant to express herself, did not believe it was a hoax. My mother's sister, Ellen, was more outspoken. Ellen Spendrup is a tall, large woman whose fiery red hair has turned white; she has never been known for espousing popular issues or for keeping her views to herself. After the disappearance she began making people uncomfortable in stores around the square saying, 'Well certainly I think they're dead.' Ellen had some fancy things to say about Sheriff Lawrence Rainey. She was furious that anyone in Neshoba County had pulled such a 'lousy dirty trick' and was especially irritated by the absence of local leadership."

At a time when the Klan network had succeeded in demonizing FBI agents and brainwashing a lot of people, Ellen and Florence were among the few whites willing to defy the Klan and talk to investigators. Ellen invited some of the agents to her home for dinner one night. She went to the A&P to buy groceries and while checking out, someone noticed the large amount of groceries and said, "You must be having a family reunion." Whereupon Ellen announced for all to hear that she was having the FBI for dinner.

One night the Klan held a meeting at the courthouse in the big courtroom on the second floor to talk about ways to drive the civil rights workers out of town. Ellen and Florence went to the meeting. Ellen took out her checkbook and faked it as if she were writing checks. She was taking notes and recording all the names of people she and Florence recognized. They turned the notes over to the FBI as well as other information they had learned.

Florence began having various health problems in the 1980s and 1990s, including Bell's Palsy, diabetes and congestive heart failure. She suffered a stroke which confined her to a wheelchair in her last few years.

Dr. Carolyn Goodman, mother of Andrew Goodman, went to Philadelphia, Mississippi in 2000 to pay Florence a visit. They had not previously met. Dr. Goodman and her youngest son, David, visited Florence in 2004. David Goodman wrote of Florence: "I had read Florence's book, *Witness in Philadelphia,* and if I had not lived through that time in history in the way that I did, I would not have believed that such an outstanding member of the Neshoba County community would have been so badly treated by her 'neighbors' because all she wanted for herself and others (all others, not just a select few) was the promises embedded in our Constitutional documents.

"My mother and Florence had a lot in common. Both of them were outspoken and did not try to shape their words to necessarily please others, particularly when it came to stating what political point of view they held. My mother told me many times that she admired Florence because she was not terrorized by an immoral majority who wanted to shut her up. . . . I am sorry that neither my mother, nor Florence lived long enough to see Barack Obama elected the 44th President of the United States, 44 years after Andrew, James and Michael were found dead in a ditch 44 days after they were first taken from us."

Florence lived to see a Neshoba County jury convict Edgar Ray Killen, the mastermind behind the ambush of the three Civil Rights workers, of manslaughter 41 years to the day of the murders.

People around the courthouse had been surprised to see Florence at the trial of Edgar Ray Killen. It was generally known that she was confined to her home in failing health. One day, minutes before court was to begin, spectators in the room reduced their talking to a quiet hum. They suddenly became aware of a voice outside the courtroom talking nonstop. The door in the back of the room opened and Florence, still talking, was wheeled in by two attendants. One thing she was heard to say was "I've been with this case too long to miss this." She had left her sick bed to be present.

Florence was again, at least symbolically, in dialogue with the people of Neshoba County. This time things were different. She saw a jury convict the man who plotted and arranged the murders. Killen was sentenced to 60 years—20 years for each murder, the sentences to run consecutively.

When Florence Mars died on April 23, 2006 at the age of 83, her obituary was published in the national media, including the New York Times, the Washington Post and the Los Angeles Times.

Among those paying tribute to Florence at the time of her death was Betty Pearson, a long time friend who probably knew her better than anyone else. Betty Pearson, of Sumner, Mississippi, was Mars' roommate at Millsaps College. "She was my oldest and dearest friend," Pearson said. "She and I met as freshmen in the fall of 1941 and have been friends ever since." They shared similar value systems, she said. "We were both sort of rebels in a sense. A little more liberal than most of the people we were with," Pearson said.

The roommates enjoyed doing many of the same things and especially shared a love for tennis, playing almost every morning before classes. An avid photographer, Florence had an artist's eye, Betty Pearson said, noting that many of her photographs are now in the Mississippi Department of Archives and History in Jackson. Betty remembered getting press passes for her and Florence to attend the Emmet Till trial in Sumner, Mississippi in 1955. "A lot of her photographs from that trial are in the archives and later during the civil rights era in the 'sixties, she took a lot of good photographs and they are there too."

Betty Pearson recalled her friend's courage, especially when she took a stand after the three civil rights workers were murdered: "She took all kinds of flak but stayed true to what she believed was right. I think Philadelphia should be really proud of her. I think now that most people in Philadelphia and across the whole state of Mississippi regret a lot of things that happened like those murders there, like the Emmet Till case, like people getting beat up trying to register to vote. All those injustices, she stood up at the time they happened and was as brave as she could be."

Civil rights activists like the Reverend Clinton Collier, who was 96 at the time Florence died, was saddened to learn of her death. He compared her work during the civil rights struggle with that of Dr. Martin Luther King: "She is an angel, a woman who I had a lot of respect for," Collier said, recalling how Florence came to his home in Neshoba County on numerous occasions after the murders. "That little woman stood up when white folks would not have dared to come out to my house," he said. "Only Dr. King can match her in my judgment. She didn't have the same job he had but she had what she had."

At Florence's memorial service on April 27, 2006, the New York Times wrote, "Ms. Mars was vindicated not only by her friends but also by her foes. At her funeral service Mr. Stanley Dearman, former editor of The Neshoba Democrat, said, "People said Florence was right; people who don't remember how they acted."

David Goodman put it succinctly: "God Bless Florence Mars, and may her memory remain forever as one of the very great Americans who had blessed us with their grace and presence on this great earth of ours."

Constance Iona Slaughter-Harvey

"I had to stand on my tiptoes in order to be seen
during our graduation picture because there
appeared to be a deliberate attempt to conceal me
as a member of the 1970 graduating class of the
University of Mississippi Law School."

*Constance Iona Slaughter-Harvey was the first African American female
to graduate from the University of Mississippi Law School. She is a former
Assistant Secretary of State of Mississippi, author and columnist for the Scott
County Times. She served on the Governor's Minority Advisory Committee, as
Regional Presidential Team Coordinator for Jimmy Carter, as Fair Hearings
Officer for Mississippi Health Planning and Development Agency, as a
Presidential Scholars Commissioner, as Executive Director of the Governor's
Office of Human Development in the Administration of Governor William
Winter, as Head of the Mississippi State Democratic Party Coordinating
Campaign and currently is in private law practice in Forest, Mississippi.*

I grew up in rural Mississippi, one of six girls, with seven years between the oldest and the youngest. Together we were known as the "Six C's"— Cheryl, Constance, Charlotte, Cynthia, Clarice and Carolyn. In fact, my parents named the store they ran as the Six Cees Superette. I maintained the name of the store building after purchasing it in 1977 for my law practice. It is known as the Six Cees Law Office Building.

As a youngster, I worked by helping my father raise pigs to sell. Rather than purchase feed, I negotiated an arrangement with the school cafeteria where I would take their "slop" and carry "slop buckets" each morning and afternoon to the farm in order to feed the pigs. For me, this behavior was part of a business to earn money, and while most of the students mocked and laughed and called me "Pigpen" and other names, the teasing did not bother me because I was looking at the big picture. When the students realized their mocking did not affect me, they stopped calling me names. This experience was helpful later in life when I walked past white males at the University of Mississippi who laughed at me and mocked me. It didn't bother me then either, because I was looking at the bigger picture—this time not for the profit from selling pigs, but the law degree.

I was viewed by my parents as the outspoken, fearless one, taking risks even at an early age. As children, we were encouraged to behave, for fear our misdeeds would be shared during our Saturday morning family "court sessions." Father "held court" by reviewing our behavior and activities for the week, and often we had to defend ourselves. I looked forward to these sessions; I seldom had to defend myself, but was always available to "represent" my sisters. I found these experiences to be educational and realized that they influenced my career choice. They also helped me to develop a sense of justice and fair play. As I grew older, I inherited my parents' intense dislike for discrimination and developed great sympathy for the underdog.

I came of age during a revolution, a bloody and painful revolution which left physical and spiritual scars on a generation of Americans that are now only beginning to heal. My revolution was the civil rights movement and one of the most challenging battlefields was Oxford, Mississippi, home of the University of Mississippi School of Law, which I entered in 1967 as one of three black female law students and where I would graduate 2-1/2 years later as the first African American female law school graduate.

The 1967 journey to the University of Mississippi Law School was interesting and challenging, but the experience of being a student there was, in retrospect, both scary and intimidating. Several days after I moved into the graduate dorm, Rick's Hall, I was almost pushed off the sidewalk by a white Nazi-looking male who refused to move over when he approached black people. On several occasions, he and I were walking on the sidewalk and met each other. Neither moved, and we bumped and continued to walk. He later learned that I was not afraid of bumping him really hard, and, after a small fight, he eventually moved off the walk when he approached me and uttered, "Damn Nigger."

Several days after starting class, I faced a barrage of insults in the library, where I sat at a table with several white male law students in order to study. One of these students, who later became a Rankin County District Attorney, turned to the others and said, "I smell a Nigger; something stinks." He then moved to another table with the others following him. I decided to join them at the other table when the same man insulted me again by saying, "The smell won't go away." This time he got up to leave and expected the others to join him, but they did not. He rushed downstairs to find another study carousel, and I decided to follow him. From that day forward, I was a target for him and he continued to hurl insults my way throughout my years at the law school. Whenever I remember his insults, my stomach tightens and I am overwhelmed by anger. I am learning, after 40 years, to move beyond that anger.

The insults continued through the remaining years of law school. My criminal procedure professor referred to a Negro defendant as a "Nigra." I could not believe I heard him correctly and asked him to repeat what he had said—not a wise thing to do under the circumstances. (I was disturbed because while I attended law school, I wanted to believe that the law was a protection for all citizens of the United States who were seen as equal under the law.) He resented my challenging him and gave me a lower grade in the class. He also taught criminal evidence and gave me a lower grade there as well. I learned in law school to expect this kind of disrespect: to be called a "Nigger," to be ignored and humiliated while I was in law school when Martin Luther King, Jr. was assassinated in 1968. I recall the tears in my soul, if not in my eyes, at the outright celebration that ensued among some of my white classmates. I recall fighting, physically and verbally, with them during that time.

Following law school, I encountered further insults in the practice of law. In May, 1970, I went to the Rankin County Jail located at the back of the court house in order to meet with 22 students from the Pearl McLauren High School who had been arrested because they attempted to convince the administration that the birthday of Dr. Martin Luther King, Jr. should be recognized and celebrated. The demonstration led to their arrest, and they were placed in the Rankin County Jail with hardened and convicted criminals without notification to their parents.

At the time I was a young staff attorney with the Lawyers Committee for Civil Rights Under Law (LCCRUL) and was contacted by activist Jim Harvey to represent these youngsters and get them out of jail. When I arrived, Jim said he was looking for "a real attorney." I advised him that I was an attorney and gained his respect when we were successful in getting the children out of prison with the promise they would be in court the following morning. (Later, Jim Harvey became my husband.)

In preparing the briefs to help these youngsters, other LCCRUL attorneys and I prepared documents removing the case from the state court to the federal court, where we believed we would have a fairer chance at success. We arrived at the court house the next morning with the intention of informing the judge that he no longer had jurisdiction of this case as it had been moved to federal court. When I stood to advise the court of the change, the judge told me to sit down and announced, "Nigger, if you get out of that seat, I will have the sheriff arrest you." I was shocked and could not believe that a judge would use such an insulting term in a court of law. I was half way out of my seat when I realized that I was the only attorney these youngsters had to represent them. My eyes were burning with anger, my nostrils widened, and heat burned my face, but I did sit down. The judge appeared to be relieved. I was told later that my eyes "pierced his racist face" and he appeared to be shaken. When the court was recessed, I told one of the judge's friends that "That bastard might call me a 'Nigger,' but I'd be damned if he'll call me 'Nigger' from the bench again."

I was surprised to learn that my parents and friends had voted for this judge who they felt was "O.K.," but he had never faced an African American attorney in his courtroom. Perhaps he had seen black people as witnesses, jailers or janitors, but never as an attorney. In fact, until that time, there had never been an African American juror or attorney in that courtroom.

I had another occasion to appear before this racist judge in my home town, before he retired. There were a number of cases in which I was the only African American attorney to appear before him. He told me to have a seat and he would call me at the end of the day after he finished with all the other lawyers. By that time, I had had enough of him and his racist attitude, so I stood and walked out of his courtroom. I went to my office; the sheriff, who had been ordered to have me return to the courtroom, contacted me, but I told him I was not returning. This sheriff understood political realities and told the judge he was not about to commit political suicide by forcing me to return. The judge was later forced to retire and had charges filed against him by a white female client accusing him of making sexual advances toward her. It is my belief that racism is an illness, which if untreated can totally destroy any semblance of life. The judge died several months later.

All of these incidents of insult and humiliation pale by comparison to knowing that my parents had to add to their prayers every night that I would not be murdered by one of several people making serious death threats against me. One never quite recovers from the image of one's Godly mother kneeling in tears to pray that the life of her child be spared when that child was engaged simply in the pursuit of bettering herself and her race through channels guaranteed by the Constitution and by principles of basic human decency.

My father was the football, basketball and track coach at Harris Junior College in Meridian, Mississippi, and also at Hawkins High School, where he taught math and social studies. Following my graduation in 1963 as valedictorian from E. T. Hawkins High School, a segregated school at the time, Daddy became principal of the North Scott Attendance Center. In 1977, the year I was married, my father became the first African American to be elected alderman in Forest, Mississippi. My father later became president of the Scott County NAACP Branch, a position he held until his death in 1981, following a fall which broke his neck. The city council meeting was held at the foot of his hospital bed and that was Daddy's last meeting. He died three days later.

In his memory, I keep Daddy's poll tax receipt for 1954 on my desk. It is a constant reminder of our painful past and the need to encourage youth to remain vigilant and to continue to vote. The Voting Rights Act was a stimulus for racial progress and empowerment of African American citizens. (I shudder to think of a world without the Voting rights Act.)

Mama was a very religious woman; God played an important role in her life. I remember her looking toward the heavens, declaring God her creator and insisting that we be compassionate and caring. She was always soft spoken and often shared what we had with people who had even less. My father was the same in his generosity, giving his last $5.00 to a woman even though she owed him $50.00 for groceries. At the time, he was wheelchair bound after losing a leg to diabetes. Both of my parents were so generous and so giving to us that we learned to be compassionate and sympathetic to others. As an example, Mama would divide one chicken among the eight of us and she took delight and joy in eating the back part. Mama was extremely articulate, well read, and a lover of words and the pen. Her writing always mesmerized me and her penmanship was perfect.

Following my graduation from high school, I attended Tougaloo College, where I met Medgar Evers six days before his life was snuffed out in its prime. I consider those six days pivotal in my life during which time I heard him say what my parents had been saying all my life: "Right is right." There may be a double standard for justice, but there is a single definition. Medgar Evers was committed and compassionate and I would have followed him almost anywhere. Six days after I met him, I witnessed and participated in Medgar Evers' funeral march; in November of that same year, President John F. Kennedy was assassinated. My freshman year was one during which the philosophy of "We Shall Overcome" was shaken and tested and finally burned indelibly into the fabric of my spirit.

I consider 1963 the defining year of my childhood and would consider 1967 and 1970 the two most disheartening years for a proud young African American woman who still experiences great pain reliving those years. Two similar events occurred, one in 1967 and one in 1970, that continue to cause heartache and disillusionment when I consider the "bigger picture." The first occurred in 1967 when I was president of the Tougaloo College student body and arranged for a group of students to be transported by professors in their cars to a rally in downtown Jackson in support of the student body at Jackson State College, now Jackson State University, in which an African American man, Benjamin Brown, had been killed by a highway patrolman in what I considered an officially sanctioned act of murder.

Tougaloo is a private, historically African American College, and Jackson State is Mississippi's largest state supported historically African American University. All of this occurred during a time when some older African American educational leaders thought it better to "soft pedal" civil rights, but many of my generation did not have it within us to soft pedal. I had arranged with the professors to transport us back to the college, but the Jackson chief of police issued a 6:00 p.m. curfew and threatened to arrest all of us if we were not off the streets before 6:00 p.m. The curfew imposed did not correspond with the transportation schedule planned, so another student and I took the Tougaloo College bus and loaded it with Tougaloo College students for the demonstration. When we returned to campus and pulled up to the gate, my heart sank. The college president was personally blocking the entrance, demanding that all of the students file off the bus. I refused to comply because I knew that all of the students would be expelled, so we drove right through the gate to the back of the campus to discharge the students from the bus in order to protect their identity. Two identities were well known to the president. I was one, and the second was the driver of the bus, Bennie Thompson, who currently serves as the second African American elected since reconstruction to the U.S. House of Representatives from Mississippi. He has served as Chairman of the Homeland Security Committee.

As a result of my "misbehavior," I was told that I could not graduate from the college. However, because of the great student support of my situation, through class boycotts and the closing of the Tougaloo College Gate, the college finally allowed me to graduate, but would not allow me to march. I was devastated because I could not understand the actions and behaviors of some of my own leaders, those to whom I had entrusted my educational future. I was eventually awarded my diploma in 1991 and marched as marshal at my mother's insistence. Daddy never saw me march at his alma mater. (I was a 4th generation Tougaloo graduate. My great-grandmother, Anna Battle Hayden, graduated from Tougaloo Daniel Hand School; my grandmother, Fannie Jane Hayden (Slaughter) graduated from Tougaloo High School; and my father, W. L. Slaughter, graduated from Tougaloo College. Note: my daughter, Constance Olivia Slaughter Harvey (Burwell) graduated from Tougaloo College in 2000.)

The second event occurred in 1970 after my graduation from the University of Mississippi School of Law. At that time there was a tragic event at Jackson State University resulting in the murders of Philip Gibbs and James Earl Green and the wounding of at least 10 others when Mississippi Highway Safety Patrolmen (MHSP) and Jackson Police Department (JPD) officers fired bullets into Alexander Hall during a demonstration. I considered that, with many others, to be the "Jackson State Massacre." I shudder at the inhumanity of the wanton shooting by officers when I think of the insane actions by youth who blast and shoot at and into crowds at schools, churches, malls, etc. In 1970, the university administration would again make the attempt to muzzle me and construct obstacles preventing the effective representation of my clients. I was hurt and angered by the actions of the administration to impede my efforts, but I was more hurt by their inaction which, in my opinion, reflected their lack of courage and anger over the killings.

When the incident at Tougaloo occurred in 1967, I was just a college student with no degrees, no credentials, not even a complete grasp of my civil rights. However, with the Jackson State Massacre in 1970, I returned, armed with a law degree. It was my intention to fight my battles with dignity in the courtroom instead of taking to the streets, which I considered my only option in 1967. However, the university officials issued an order that I was to be barred from campus. Even though I was the legal representative for the families of the two male students killed at Jackson State, a federal court order had to be obtained for me to enter the campus and review the evidence at Alexander Hall, the site of the barrage of gunfire that resulted in the deaths of my two clients. Philip Gibbs was a 20 year old junior from the small Mississippi town of Ripley and James Earl Green was a 17 year old high school student from Jackson who made the innocent but fatal decision to cut through campus on his way home from work.

At one point during my investigation, I was intimidated by being placed in a police car and threatened with arrest, a frightening experience indeed for any person of color at that time, but I persevered and overcame this obstacle in filing the lawsuit. When we lost the case at trial in federal court in 1972, I was saddened. I expected the white racist establishment to react as it did, but I expected African American leaders to be outraged. When my own people stood in my way of winning, however, it pierced my heart just as the incident at Tougaloo had done several years earlier. Other events in my legal career have made me angry, but few have made me cry. I shed tears over this incident—tears for a society which would officially sanction murder, and tears for those of my own race who refused to call it what it was.

In retrospect, I believe that these events strengthened me, for I became adamantly determined that no other student would feel my sense of betrayal. The actions of the administrators had not been explained to me and had they been, it would have greatly lessened my pain. A person can agree to disagree peacefully when she knows what page the other person is on, but neither of these educators, both of whom did a great deal of good for their respective institutions, bothered to even tell me from what book we were reading. From those experiences which gave me purpose, I also learned that communication is one of the most important gifts we can share with our children. We must always take the time to tell our children why.

Mama was a very educated woman who loved to read, to compose poetry and write plays. When I was a student at the university, Mama wrote a prayer asking God to protect and keep me. That poem, written in pencil on notebook paper, keeps me focused and on target. She wrote;

> Her gray-flecked head bowed downward
> As she humbly began her day
> Her worried black hands reached heavenward
> And she was heard to say
>
> O, dear God, my child's face is black
> Black as a blackbird's wing!
> So God please be merciful
> And let her young heart sing.
>
> The inhuman deeds of the past century
> Press heavily upon her back;
> To be free she cries and struggles, Lord
> Ere her poor spirits crack.
>
> Now of your loving grace and wisdom, Lord
> Kindly give her a share
> And I shall rest and smile dear God
> For You and she are a pair.
>
> (To Constance, From Mama, 10/11/67)

It was during Daddy's illness that I realized Mama's strength as she became our family's backbone by providing prayers, comfort and compassion. Mama enjoyed helping others, especially as a manager of the Six Cees Superette, where she was the customers' favorite. It was in this role that Mama met Dick Molpus, Secretary of State of Mississippi from 1984 to 1996. He was one of her customers and would buy an orange soda and gum every morning en route to work in Morton. She was extremely fond of "this little white boy," who later became my supervisor in the Governor's office and my boss as the Secretary of State. Mama had a way of reading people and her notes were correct on Dick's page.

Daddy taught me to fight for what is right with my head, my heart, my voice, and my body, and during the turbulent years which followed my upbringing I did all of this. Mama taught me that, on some occasions it was better to speak softly than to shout. Even when we whisper, there could be strength and passion in what we say. Her lessons took me longer to learn, but they have also served me well. I sometimes think that Daddy's fire got me into the courtroom and later the halls of state government, but it has been Mama's diplomacy which has kept me there.

Based on the strength of my parents and their influence, I have developed a strong foundation that rejects inequality, mistreatment, racism and discrimination. I have serious problems accepting "my place" in society. From Mama, I learned there are times to be extremely vocal, and there are times to whisper. Wars and battles are selective. From the depth of my family's qualities of sympathy and compassion I could draw for strength and courage all my life. I cannot plot my future without recalling my past—a past profoundly shaped by two parents who taught me, first and foremost, to be true to myself and my ideals.

Many people—black and white, female and male, young and old—have influenced my life for the better, but two particular role models come to mind: The late Fannie Lou Hamer, a former sharecropper who rose to become a fearless and respected civil rights leader, whose voice rang out across America from the cotton fields of Mississippi, a leader in the Voting

Rights Movement who helped found the historic Mississippi Freedom Democratic Party (MFDP) and Medgar Evers, my male role model whose life was such an inspiration to me. I could identify with his calling and the fire in his soul that propelled him to do the right thing at the right time. I especially admired his courage and his desire to tell the truth.

Colin Powell recently said, "As we climbed on the backs of others, so must we allow our backs to be used for others to go even higher than we have." It is again time for all of us to bare our backs and bend down. We must teach our children that *I* is a word which has worth, but that *We* is a pearl of even greater price. To teach any lesson, you must first learn it. We must accept that *I* is not an end unto itself, but a valuable, indeed intrinsic, part of *We*—*We* being African Americans, *We* being women, and finally, *We* being the entire family of people.

I was very taken with the Reverend Dr. Martin Luther King, Jr., and his speech about the mountaintop. Mountains are an excellent symbol for my struggle at the University of Mississippi School of Law. Mountains are rugged terrain with very steep grades that are difficult to climb. The higher you climb, the more changeable and unpredictable the conditions you will find.

At the university, by the Grace of God, I did journey to the mountaintop and stick my flag into the rocky dirt of the future. I had to climb over the past and the present to get there. Occasionally, since then, I have felt that we have nothing before us as I tried cases in front of prejudiced judges and juries that had determined the verdict before I even spoke. But mostly, I feel now, when I reach deep down inside myself, that we have everything before us and that the promised land of social justice is a real place that will one day be reached—rather than a hollow ideal for which so many have sacrificed so much. To sacrifice in vain would simply be more irony than I could stand, so I wake up every day with my compass in hand and share my map with all who will follow it.

What we have accomplished is indeed much more than lovely. It is real, lasting and abiding. It will be here to tell our story when we are gone, but the challenges, the unrealized potential, the unrighted wrongs are dark and deep. I believe that if left unmet, the challenges which remain could one day overtake the good to which my parents and their parents dedicated their lives. I am unwilling to stand idly by and watch that happen. I hope that my sisters and brothers of all races, especially my daughter, Constance Olivia and son-in-law, James Burwell, will join me in moving forward.

Joan Mulholland

"What were we trying to change?—Everything!"

Joan Mulholland, public school teacher, Arlington, Virginia, one of the early white southern civil rights activists, remembers the struggles involved in Mississippi in the early 1960s.

I am southern and white—as southern as the red clay of Georgia, as southern as Lee's Mansion overlooking the Potomac. Northern Virginia is where I live and rural Georgia was "down home." My great-grandparents were slave owners in Georgia. My great-grandfather and his four brothers fought in the Army of the Confederacy to defend their homeland.

My grandmother's generation was essentially made up of internal refugees who became sharecroppers. My mother escaped dirt floor poverty and made her way to Washington, DC, in the 1930s, looking for that "good government job." My father, from a solidly middle class Iowa family, came with the same goal. My parents met on the midnight shift of a New Deal agency in the Old Post Office Building.

As a young child, I lived in a new garden apartment complex in Arlington, Virginia, with a good school and park nearby. My special weekly treat was walking to the drugstore with my dad for a chocolate ice cream cone. (He loved ice cream—I suspect I was just his excuse to get some!) There were Saturday movies at the Buckingham Theater, tap and ballet lessons in the Community House, Brownie and Girl Scout activities and trips to Woodies and Garfinkle's (Washington's premier department stores)—all strictly segregated by law and custom.

African Americans were just part of the background scenery of my young life. Yes, "they" came to our homes as cleaning women, might operate elevators and serve food (both in uniforms) and were seen doing dirty jobs. It was common knowledge that they were "different"—not too smart, dirty, disease-carrying, in need of "help" (like our castoffs). As far as I knew, they didn't have full names. The "whys" of all this weren't discussed. It was just the way things were, the way God made "them"—and the boogeyman was always black (a caution to little children!).

I remember:

- Sturdy brick schools for white children and shabby schools that looked like a strong wind would knock them off their stone pilings for black children.
- Discussions at my grandmother's house in Georgia about whether or not a particular lynching victim was guilty of a crime, but no discussion about whether lynching was right or wrong.
- A white Army officer's house in Arlington, Virginia, being fire-bombed because he invited a fellow black Army officer to his house—they had been stationed together in Germany.
- My mother locking the car doors when we drove through the black Halls Hill area and telling my sister and me not to look at the people in the car stopped next to us at the light because they were Negroes.
- Massive Resistance (Virginia's response to the Supreme Court's *Brown vs. Board of Education* decision on segregated schools) closing schools in part of the state and my fear that it could happen here and I wouldn't have a high school diploma.
- Flyers advertising Klan meetings nailed to telephone poles on Glebe Road in Arlington in 1965.

In Sunday school, we sang, "Jesus loves the little children . . . red and yellow, black and white, they are precious in his sight . . ." We memorized "Inasmuch as ye have done it unto one of the least of these my Brethren, ye have done it unto me," and "Do unto others as you would have them do unto you." I heard about the brotherhood of man all the time, but we certainly did not practice it.

All that began to change for me when I was in high school. Our church youth group was joined one Sunday evening by a few students from the black high school. As I understood it at the time, the visit was arranged by the minister and the black YMCA, but the visit was shrouded in secrecy. We knew these guests were coming, but we were not to tell anyone, even our parents, for fear of reprisals—from police, church deacons, the local Nazis or other irate citizens. For most (if not all) of us, having these visitors at our weekly spaghetti dinners was our first chance to have inter-racial friendships.

I began to feel that segregation had to end. Treating people as less than human was so against the teachings of God that I could not object in private and do nothing in public. I wanted a better place for all of us, es-pecially in the South. We southerners had to put our own house in order. When the chance to do something came, I felt I must act.

I have made a sort of diary, really just short notes about some of my experiences with the civil rights movement. Here it is for you.

May, 1960

What an irony! I wanted to enroll in a small church school in Ohio. My mother said no, Duke University was where I should go. Why? Because Duke is in North Carolina—in the safely segregated South. Mother got her way and now I have been arrested for sitting in at Kress's lunch counter with Negro students from North Carolina College (NCC). A few other students from Duke (mostly male graduate students, but also my room-mate, Lucia) were arrested too—along with about 50 NCC students. The University is NOT happy! They retaliated against a divinity student who has been working as an assistant housemaster. He was told he will not have a job next year because he was arrested for his civil rights activities.

After we were bailed out, Lucia and I were called to the dean's office. The door was locked behind us and we were ordered to call our parents to tell them we had been arrested. We were not getting out of the office until we did so. It was after dark and it seemed like nobody else was in the building. The whole experience was intimidating! Lucia's scholarship was threatened, and she really needs it. Our dorm counselor told us we have "deep underlying problems" and should see a psychiatrist or psychologist. On the brighter side, my English teacher said that if I were in jail when he gave a big test, he would bring it down to the jail because he knew I couldn't cheat in the cell. He then gave me a big friendly smile. I heard that a lot of the faculty really supports what we are doing. I do not think I want to come back to this school in September.

October, 1960

What a summer! I returned to Washington, DC, and made contact with some Howard University students who called themselves NAG (for the Nonviolent Action Group). They were planning to bring the sit-in movement to lunch counters in Arlington—my home town. I joined them in their efforts; there we were heckled by teenagers who came for their after-school snacks and were angry when they found the counter closed. The first night quite a crowd gathered outside the drugstore. It was pretty tense at closing time. The big question for me was what the American Nazi Party would do. Their headquarters is in Arlington. With their arm bands, German shepherds and threatening reputation, I had to wonder what action they would take. Of course, they showed up the very first day and got right behind us, wearing swastika armbands and picketing. They said some quite nasty things to us as well. Outside the store they handed out flyers claiming Jews were behind integration. On a positive note, some white people expressed support for us. It took about two weeks of demonstrations until Arlington's eateries opened to black customers.

Next we moved across the river to Maryland to try to desegregate Glen Echo Amusement Park (white Washington's summer playground). I bought some ride tickets and passed them on to Negro students for use on the merry-go-round. (How can one ride on the "back" of a merry-go-round?) The Negro students made it to the merry-go-round, climbed up on the animals and then were all arrested. We picketed for the rest of the hot humid summer, as did the Nazis. The local white community came out to support us. They made signs and gave us sandwiches. They took us into their homes for breaks and joined us on the picket line. But Glen Echo ended the season still segregated. Perhaps it will change in the spring.

February, 1961

I have decided to apply to a Negro college in the South, or rather to several of them. If I do not get accepted, I will understand, given the violence of

angry whites where Negro students have enrolled at white schools. The
Negro administrators may think that admitting a white student is too
risky for their campus and their students, but I'll have reached out in
friendship. If I get admitted, I will go on and get my degree.

What happened to Charlayne Hunter at the University of Georgia
brought me to this decision and encouraged me to apply to a southern tra-
ditionally black college. Both Charlayne Hunter and Hamilton Holmes
have been admitted to the University of Georgia, but were forced to leave
twice. The pictures of Charlayne clutching her Madonna on the night of
the riot, when the police used tear gas, especially moved me. These were
my people doing this to her, a young lady about my age. What could I do
to show that not all white southerners were racist? My idea was to return
to school at a Negro college in the South, but not in Georgia where my
relatives might suffer for my behavior. My SNCC friends say that students in Mississippi haven't gotten a movement together and it would be
a good place for me to go. So, I applied to Tougaloo College, just north
of Jackson, Mississippi. It is a small accredited church school just like the
one I wanted in the first place.

Why am I doing this? Because I'm a southerner and school segregation
is a big problem in the South. We need to solve the problem by having
better schools for everyone, not by closing them as they did in Virginia or
rioting to force out the people we don't want to attend. Doesn't Christianity
teach us to treat people the way we want to be treated and to love our
neighbors as ourselves? Besides, having two school systems, even when
one is second class, is expensive. It is better to have one really good school
system for all.

June 6, 1961

I'm leaving tomorrow on the Freedom Rides. It's not just riding buses
anymore. Now the focus has shifted from bloody Alabama to Jackson,
Mississippi. People will come from different directions and by different
conveyances. My group will fly to New Orleans, get some non-violent
training and take the train to Jackson. Six more people from NAG are

going as well, including that pontificating Stokely Carmichael. What a New Yorker! When Hank Thomas (one of the NAG guys) left on the Freedom Ride last May, the idea was to test compliance with a recent Supreme Court decision barring segregation in interstate travel facilities (like bus stations).

We sort of joked that he was getting a free summer vacation even though we knew it was potentially dangerous. When we saw the pictures with him by the burning bus outside Anniston, Alabama, and the Freedom Riders beaten so badly in Birmingham, we responded with action. Part of the non-violent belief is that when someone falls, others step forward to take their place. Paul, Dion and John were the first to go. I got a middle-of-the-night call from Paul, from the basement of the church in Montgomery where everyone was trapped by the mob, saying to send down more people. All three were on those first buses into Jackson. Everyone was promptly arrested, so the goal became to fill the jails until interstate travel was open to everyone. The Kennedys aren't happy with this, but the Supreme Court has already ruled. It is a matter of enforcing the law! Several other NAG folks have already gone, and I hope more will follow.

I got a letter of acceptance from Tougaloo College, even though my high school refused to send them a transcript (and the counselor was real specific why!). I'll stay in jail as long as I can and still make it to school on time.

October, 1961

Everyone was arrested for our non-violent protest, placed in the Jackson City Jail and moved to Hinds County Jail after we were convicted. There were 17 of us in the white women's cell, sleeping under the bunks and in the dripping shower. So, we were transferred from Hinds County Jail to the maximum security unit at Parchman, the notorious state penitentiary in the Delta. For the women, it was a physical improvement. The food was a little better, the place was newer and cleaner, and there were only two of us to a cell (with bunk beds, commode and sink). Death Row had been cleared out to make room for us. I heard the guys had it a lot tougher.

The hard part was the total isolation in the worst jail in the worst state in the nation. No yelling out the window for passers-by to hear. Once a week or so one of the attorneys came to see us. More Freedom Riders were being brought in and people were being bailed out. (You had 39 days to post bond if you were going to appeal your case.) We were getting a little news from the outside world from our lawyers and from the new arrivals. Mail in and out was restricted and censored.

Rabbi Perry Nussbaum, from Jackson, Mississippi (at considerable risk to himself), visited faithfully. Anyone who wished could go to his prayer sessions. I was one of the faithful. He worked messages from home and world news into the Hebrew prayers and sent form letters to our families reassuring them.

Food was monotonous and "southern," but what would you expect? On the 4th of July we got fried chicken and lemonade. It was a real treat, especially since Mississippi did not celebrate the holiday until after World War II (Vicksburg fell to the Yankees on the 4th of July and fireworks never made it there on time anyway—they were saved until New Year's).

I served my two months (later people got six months) and part of my $200 fine was served at $3.00 per day. The attorneys then paid off the rest of the fine and got me out of jail just before school started in September. The whole summer, room and board, compliments of the State of Mississippi!

I had hidden a diary in the hem of my skirt while we were in the Hinds County Jail. It was still there when I got my clothes back at the time of release.

Tougaloo College is a welcome relief after Parchman and getting back to classes is good for me. I'm living in a dorm room with three other girls. It is sort of crowded, but we get along. They were a bit surprised to see me, but not nearly as surprised as a girl who saw me that first night coming down the dimly lit hallway to the bathroom in my pale pink shorty pajamas. She thought she was seeing a ghost!

People seem to be accepting me as they see that I have to study hard just like they do. Being from the South, we have things in common across racial lines. (In the county jail, I felt much closer to the Negro Freedom Riders—mostly from schools in the South—than to my white Yankee cell mates.) The school has a beautiful setting—big oak trees with Spanish moss and plenty of space between buildings. It's a few miles north of Jackson, sort of isolated and rural. It's also very welcoming to the civil rights movement. When all the Freedom Riders who were out on bail had to return to Jackson last August for court appearances, they stayed at Tougaloo College. The college is supported by northern churches and does not have to worry about state funding. The charter predates the state's segregation laws and does not mention race—that's one reason they admitted me (and another white girl who is just down for one semester). I like it here. I'm pretty sure I'll stay and graduate.

December, 1963

The year 1963 stands out as both a national high point and, to borrow a phrase, the "year that will live in infamy." I think most people will remember 1963 as the year of the March on Washington, D.C. For me, this event was an extraordinary moment, surrounded by violence and tragedy. I spent the summer of 1963 working in the press section of the March on Washington's Planning Office in D.C. We worried the government troops or violent opposition would keep the March from happening. I remember on the morning of the March, some of us went over to the mall and how calm, beautifully calm, it was.

The spring had been anything but calm. The Children's Crusade in Birmingham had been met with fire hoses, with bone-breaking water pressure, and police dogs. Police dogs are my personal least favorite form of intimidation.

Jackson had its lunch counter sit-in. Lois Chaffee, a young white woman who works at Tougaloo, and I really weren't supposed to be part of the demonstration. We were "spotters" for the picket line down the street—there to watch what happened and call in reports to Medgar Evers' NAACP office. The picketers were arrested immediately, so we went to Woolworth's to see how the sit-in was going. Three of my classmates—Anne Moody, Pearlena Lewis and Memphis Norman—took seats at the counter. Soon an increasingly hostile crowd, mostly students from the nearby high school, gathered behind them. After Memphis was kicked senseless and arrested, the girls became separated. Lois and I took seats at the counter with each of the girls to provide moral support and a bit of safety in numbers (it's easier to beat up one person than two). During the next hour or so, several others, both black and white, joined us. We were victims of verbal and physical abuse, including taunts, having mustard, ketchup, and sugar dumped on us, and lit cigarettes pressed on to our skin. The expression, "the roar of the crowd," took on a whole new meaning. After several others joined us, the mob of high schoolers grew and started trashing the store. Finally, the manager closed the place.

Our college president heard the news on the radio and came down. He convinced the police to give us safe passage on the sidewalk outside so cars could pick us up and take us back to Medgar Evers' (the statewide NAACP leader) office. Two weeks later he was shot dead in his driveway as he returned home from a civil rights mass meeting. Things in Jackson went downhill from there.

The March on Washington was a moment of hope—but it didn't last long. Less than three weeks later, a church in Birmingham was bombed on Sunday morning. Four girls, just 11 to 14 years old, were killed. A group of us from Tougaloo went to the funeral for three of them. That day is my saddest memory (so far) from the civil rights movement. The church was packed. Loudspeakers carried the service to the crowds in the street. Dr. Martin Luther King, Jr., spoke, and the caskets were carried down the steps to the hearse. I was there with a group of civil rights workers from Tougaloo. Lots of student activists came. Those girls who died had been getting ready for a church youth day program. We all knew it could be any one of us at any time.

May, 1964

I'll get my degree in a few days, in history because it had three fewer hours math requirements than sociology. Going to Tougaloo was an excellent choice. I've gotten a good education and I've been very involved with the civil rights movement, especially SNCC, the entire time I've been in Mississippi. Because of the obvious danger to everyone of having white women out in public, I did a lot of office work and out-of-public-view things. One way or another, I had a part in just about everything, including voter registration, visits to white churches, the downtown boycott, putting out the Mixissippi News (a newsletter for and about SNCC workers around the state), the ongoing Freedom Rider trials, visits to the campus by everyone from Dr. Martin Luther King, Jr., Ralph Bunche (Nobel Peace Prize winner), Pete Seeger, Bob Dylan and northern white students on spring break, fund raising, the cultural boycott of events in Jackson, especially at the city auditorium (with performers canceling their appearances) and a concert at Tougaloo by Joan Baez as an alternative event.

Reflecting Back

Why did we sit in? We sat in because it was an approach that went directly to the heart of the matter. We wanted service *there,* at the lunch counter. It was "direct action," not "indirect," like a long legal route through the courts or meeting after meeting after meeting. It was also "non-violent"—it confronted an evil practice with an assertive but non-retaliatory practice. It did not "attack" anybody, but it helped the other person confront and deal with the problem directly and hopefully from within their soul.

What were we trying to change? In one word: Everything. The lunch counters were just one place that needed changing. They were particularly visible and aggravating because students—or anybody—could shop anywhere else in the store, even buy food to carry out, but when it came to sitting down to eat, the rules changed. The lunch counters were a symbol, but the problem was everywhere from the maternity wards at the hospital to the graveyard.

The South had been changing slowly—from Truman's desegregation of the Armed Forces to *Brown v. Board of Education* to the Montgomery Bus Boycott—bit by bit change *was* taking place. The sit-ins galvanized the students and spread like wildfire. Change began to break out everywhere, not just in the area of discrimination, but in the minds and hearts of people who found a new strength, new ways to think about the status quo and a new way to exercise power. This was not just on the question of racial discrimination, but on all kinds of problems worldwide. "We shall overcome" has become an anthem of change everywhere.

The "lessons" of the sit-ins and the civil rights movement are still with me. Things I had to think through or deal with then about fear and friendship, steadfastness, "keeping your eyes on the prize," being open to truth—were important in what I wanted for my own children. I tried to pass my values on to them. Not that they had to deal with the exact same problems as my generation, but that they could apply these concepts to the problems facing their generation.

Looking back, I can see the tremendous differences those years have made in my life. The way my five sons chose their school friends (and their wives) reflects the experience of my college days. Gatherings of family and close friends resemble a United Nations potluck! Community and neighborhood school issues find me drawing on Mississippi perspectives and skills. For 30 years I worked in the local elementary schools, firm in the belief that every child had something to offer his classmates and that we all benefitted from knowing each other. The child from the shelter, the embassy kid, the newly arrived refugee, or the congressman's offspring are equal in the most important ways—and in the eyes of God. Sometimes I surprised myself by how much required curriculum I could work in around ideas of getting to know and appreciate each other. My love of travel came from my father, but my penchant for feeling at home wherever I am and getting involved in the community, making lasting friends and incorporating it all into who I am, clearly comes from my experiences at Tougaloo. I hate to think what I'd have missed if I'd stayed at Duke!

I left Mississippi in May, 1964 after receiving my degree from Tougaloo, shortly before the beginning of Freedom Summer. It was time for me to leave; I had come as a student and now I had completed my studies. I returned to Arlington, Virginia—in the last half century it has become a very different place from where I grew up. We're no longer a sleepy "white" suburb, but a diverse urban center in our own right. Medgar Evers is among the heroes buried on the grounds of Robert E. Lee's old home down by the river. Some days I take flowers and go to his grave to reflect on what it took for America to change. There is no turning back.

June Elizabeth Johnson

"I don't care what happens to me—I'm going
to be free or continue to be part of a struggle to
fight for the freedom of people in this country.
I've done nothing else in my life and I intend
to do that for the rest of my life."

She was 14 years old. A young adolescent with a penchant for fairness, equality and making life better for the disenfranchised. She was 14 years old when she began attending meetings of the Student Non-Violent Coordinating Committee (SNCC) after seeing a flyer announcing a mass meeting at one of the local churches. She was 14 years old when she began a career of civil rights activism which she would follow for the rest of her life. She was June Johnson, born in Greenwood, Mississippi on December 31, 1947 to Lula Bell Johnson and Theoda Johnson, Sr. June Johnson was one of 12 children and was raised by her maternal grandmother, Emily Johnson Holt.

This chapter contains the reflections of five people invited by Lawrence Guyot, a prominent leader in the civil rights movement, who knew and loved June Elizabeth Johnson. They admired her courage and dedication to freedom. They carry her torch today.

Rose Freeman Massey, a high school colleague of June's who joined her in the civil rights movement, was arrested with June and shared a cell with her in the Montgomery County Jail. She recalls:

June and I met in 1963. We were both still in high school. I was 17 and she was 16. We met at the Greenwood SNCC office. June taught me the ropes of canvassing the neighborhood to facilitate the flow of information. We attempted to get people to go to the courthouse to register to vote. June taught me various routes and short cuts between the SNCC office and the courthouse particularly when being chased by the police. If we were at the courthouse on the picket line and the sheriff pulled the old black bus up, she would give me the signal to head for the office so we wouldn't go to jail and on to the county farm. June knew that there was a time to "hold them" and she also knew when to "fold them."

June and I were two of the youngest people working at the SNCC office. We showed up every day because we wanted to be free. We knew that freedom was coming and it wouldn't be long. Although June was the youngest, she was the leader. She had more Movement experience and savvy than I had. She was one of the most courageous individuals that I ever had the privilege of knowing. June wasn't afraid of anything. She definitely wasn't afraid to speak truth to power. She was not afraid of the police or anyone else that was a part of the white power structure. June always stood her ground, and she taught me to do so as well. She taught me to stand up and fight for what I believed in.

Lawrence Guyot convinced June and me to attend a workshop in the Carolinas to improve our organizing skills. On the way back to Greenwood, we sat in at a lunch counter in Winona, Mississippi. We demanded to be served. The waitress refused to serve us and called the police. We were arrested and placed in the Montgomery County jail (Winona, Mississippi). June and I were cell mates. She kept telling the police officers that we had a right to be served. She stated that we were citizens of the United States of America, and that we were entitled to civil and human rights. The police officer told June to shut up. He hit her upside her head with a blackjack. Although June was bleeding from her head she kept talking. She stated that the Interstate Commerce ruling had struck down segregation in public transportation and we had a right to be served at that lunch counter. She further stated that we wanted to be free.

I was horrified, because I had never before heard any black person speak like that to a white person. The state trooper told me to wash June's dress and "there better not be any damn blood on that dress" when he returned. June said, "Come on, I will help you wash the dress because I don't want you to get hit like I did." She said these white folks are not playing. I was amazed at her courage and strength.

We got out of jail the day after Medgar Evers was assassinated. Our stay in the Montgomery County jail, the murder of Medgar Evers, the subjugation that poor blacks encountered and endured weighed heavily on June. In fact, these experiences would shape her life going forward and catapulted her into a lifetime of activism. Some people say she was driven. Others say she was an opportunist. I say she was a local girl transformed by SNCC. At fifteen June was "tired of being sick and tired." Thus she never stood down from the struggle for human rights. The world is a smaller place without June E. Johnson.

Charles McLaurin, one of the major leaders in the civil rights movement in Mississippi, recalls first meeting June Johnson during a SNCC crisis that followed a shooting incident in late summer of 1963 that seriously wounded a Tougaloo college student. This incident prompted a call for an all out show of force from SNCC workers to counter the attempt of the White Citizens Council's effort to stop SNCC's voter registration drive in LeFlore County.

At the time, June was a fourteen-year-old student at Broad Street, a local school that was located only a short distance from Greenwood's SNCC Headquarters. After school June Johnson and several other students would come by the SNCC office and lead groups of field organizers from other areas on door to door canvassing tours and introduce them to various key people in the Greenwood community. As a SNCC organizer from Sunflower County, I was assigned to work with June Johnson's voter registration canvassing team.

June Johnson's family was well known in the Greenwood community due to the fact that the family was large and their mother, Lulabell Johnson, was a strong black woman known for her strict rules and control over her girls and boys as well as her influence in her church.

June Johnson's mother at first did not find favor with her children getting involved with the "Freedom Riders," as SNCC organizers were referred to in the early days in Greenwood and the Delta. Often June and her brother, Waite, would stop by the SNCC office against their mother's advice.

June Johnson's willingness to give her time and leadership to the voters' registration effort on a regular basis made her very popular with the SNCC leadership, especially Bob Moses and Annelle Ponder, the SCLC representative. Annelle became June's mentor. Once Mrs. Lulabell Johnson met

Bob, Annelle and other SNCC staff in person, she started to feel better toward the SNCC group and soon became a strong supporter of the voter registration drive in Greenwood. Toward the end of the summer of 1963, June's entire family had become involved in SNCC and Lulabell Johnson opened her home to housing and feeding SNCC people.

When June went to her mother and asked for permission to attend a SCLC sponsored training conference in South Carolina that summer, it was because of Annelle Ponder and Bob Moses that June Johnson was able to make the trip. This trip turned out to be the beginning of a never ending nightmare for June Johnson, Annelle Ponder, Euvester Simpson and Fannie Lou Hamer. The trip was an introduction to the movement which subsequently led to the terror and brutality that June Johnson and the other women endured in a Winona, Mississippi jail in 1963. The Winona jail incident would cause 14 year old June Johnson nightmares for the rest of her life.

Between late 1963 and the early 1980s, I had limited contact with June Johnson. We met up in the early 1980s at the Elks Hall in Greenwood, Mississippi with Larry "Blue" Neal in order to discuss our concerns about the new Congressional Second District which had been recently drawn by a federal court decision. We worked together to achieve our goal of electing a black candidate to Congress from the Second District of Mississippi. We held meetings and caucuses attempting to nominate a strong black candidate to beat Republican, Webb Franklin.

Henry J. Kirksey was the expert in the battle to reconstruct the Second District in the Delta. This was a battle to determine who would represent the black population of Holmes County against Franklin. Robert Clark announced his candidacy. June and I felt bound to support our convention's choice, but we did not feel that State Representative Robert G. Clark would be the aggressive, outspoken black candidate necessary to bring a heavy black turnout which would be needed to defeat the white Republican in the newly created "Delta District."

The result of that election was a defeat for the black community in the Delta and proved that the white voters in the Mississippi Delta would not elect a black person to office. Therefore, June and I believed that to have a chance for a black candidate to be elected to Congress or to any other office in Mississippi would require at least a 65% black voting age population and a grassroots organizing effort to turn out a large black vote.

Despite our defeat at the polls, June and I were both very pleased that we had taken the action we did. Through our efforts we stimulated new voter interest in the Second Congressional District. We helped to identify a black Democratic candidate and did everything possible with our limited resources and a strong motivation to restore voting rights to black citizens in the Mississippi Delta. Mississippi had taken our black district from us when our right to vote was taken away in 1890. Since that time, black citizens, could not vote and had neither power nor protection. We viewed this opportunity as a chance to generate black interest and reclaim our Delta District.

June Johnson moved from Greenwood, Mississippi to Washington, D.C., shortly after our last SNCC adventure. Several months prior to June Johnson's untimely death on April 18, 2007, she returned to Greenwood. Although we did not have an opportunity to meet in person, we had a number of relevant and important phone conversations about the Movement and progress that had been made in civil rights.

Our goal was the election of blacks to public office in Mississippi by strengthening the development of black leadership. It is my belief that with June's strength and her commitment, we have been able to meet our goals.

John C. Brittain, a civil rights attorney from the North who worked in Mississippi during the civil rights movement, recalls June Johnson as a "Civil Rights Agitator."

When I met June Johnson around 1970 in Mississippi, I did not know about her heroine status as a 15-year-old SNCC member who was arrested and beaten by jailors for attempting to register black people to vote. However, as a new young civil rights lawyer from the north working in Mississippi, I quickly learned to respect this 22-year-old sister from Greenwood. It was the beginning of a 37-year friendship that lasted until she went home in 2007. I moved from Mississippi in 1993; we remained in touch though there were long spells without word or sight of each other. Yet, when we reunited, it was like the old days in Mississippi during which June demonstrated her courage for the cause of freedom.

During a visit to Mississippi in 1981, June gave me an enlarged reprint from a newspaper article that appeared in the Commonwealth, Greenwood, Mississippi, Sunday, June 3, 1981, p. 5. June inscribed the large poster to me as follows: ". . . for your work in the 1973 Leflore County district election suit." On the poster appears five white men and one African American woman, June Johnson, the candidates for the LeFlore County Board of Supervisors, District Three. The newspaper ran a typical pre-election question and answer article. I have kept this slightly tattered pop artwork for 27 years while moving to and living in four states. I did not quite know why I retained the artifact until I moved to the District of Columbia in 2005 and reunited with June. When I showed her the poster, she showered me with love and appreciation as we recalled her entering the race for supervisor of LeFlore County, Mississippi. She represented a threat to the ruling order in 1981 after civil rights advocates and their lawyers won the LeFlore County voting rights lawsuit that changed the method of electing supervisors to the county board.

There was June, the once militant (in the eyes of white folk) SNCC worker a decade earlier, now running for an elected county office. June was articulate, knowledgeable and "Unbought and Unbossed," to borrow from the book title by the late Shirley Chisholm, the black Congresswoman from Brooklyn, New York. For each of eight questions to the candidates, June's answers were far more comprehensive and longer than any of her five male opponents. One question illustrates her superiority to the other five candidates:

Question 6. What is your opinion on county supervisors installing culverts on private property? How many readers had ever heard of a culvert, at least outside of rural areas? A culvert is a large corrugated metal pipe often installed to fill a gully and provide a bridge for automobiles and pedestrians to cross. Members of the board of supervisors in those days used the installation of culverts as a service to constituents and to extract political power. Each of the five men had a one-sentence answer opposing culverts on private property.

However, June's written response contained six strong sentences:

"Culverts should be placed on the Right of Way on public property. I am against culverts being on private property period. However, the public must be informed as to the rare exceptional cases where culverts cannot be placed on Leflore County public property. Again, priority should go to the areas where homeowners need to travel to and fro. As you might know, the wealthy people attempt to get as many culverts placed on their property as possible; Mississippi law prohibits the placement of culverts on private property, but there are exceptions. The exceptions should favor resident homeowners who need the culvert to enhance travel."

What she meant by the word, "wealthy" were white people, and the "resident homeowners" were poor or people of moderate income—white and black—who needed culverts for travel. Hence, June intersected race and class in running for office in the Mississippi rural Delta County. Thus, she became dangerous to the ruling elite, just as did Dr. Martin Luther King.

The "Washington Post" obituary article (April 18, 2007, B6) notes that June moved from Mississippi to the District of Columbia in 1982, a year after this story about the candidates appeared. According to June (in personal conversations with me in 2005), she moved because of threats to her life in Mississippi. June Johnson, a physically tall lady, stood even higher in the legacy of Ella Baker and Fannie Lou Hamer. She was a true civil rights agitator.

Regena Lynn Thomas currently serves as the senior pastor of Bethel AME Church in Glassboro, New Jersey. She had been Secretary of State for New Jersey from 2002 through 2006, and previously served as a leading political consultant for the Democratic National Committee and for the District of Columbia Mayors Marion Barry and Sharon Pratt Kelly. Ms. Thomas was graduated from Moorehead State University in Kentucky. She presents the following recollections of her encounters with June Johnson:

June Johnson did not compromise when it came to the rights of those she believed had been unjustly treated. Physically standing head-to-head and looking into the eyes of her adversaries, she professed her passions for the issues she believed in. Relentless, she approached her subjects with the instinctive nature of a lioness protecting her young. Intact with southern dialect, moisture in her eyes that represented the tears of those she encountered in the civil rights movement, voice projection of a southern preacher and her stature that matched any concrete monument in Washington, D.C., June would begin her confrontation of the issue at hand. Yes, confrontation in the definition of face to face; however, those who found themselves on the opposite side would feel the defiance which the word confrontation invokes. Congressman, Mayor, Council member or business person; titles and/or positions did not matter to June; the rights of people, African Americans in particular, stood front and center.

Her love for her home state of Mississippi could not go undetected. One could not be in her presence long before encountering a story of a recent visit home or her childhood activism. Her love for her state could be seen in her relationship with fellow Mississippians Marion Barry, then Mayor of Washington, D.C., Congressman Bennie Thompson and civil rights and community activist Lawrence Guyot. If one did not know, it could be assumed that they were, in fact, family members. Needless to say, they received no special treatment when it came to her opinion on their position of issues that were close to her. In addition, though not from Mississippi, Congresswoman Eleanor Holmes Norton could be added to the list.

In 2004, while the Democrats were preparing to unseat President George W. Bush and finalize plans for their Democratic Convention in Boston, Massachusetts, I was in my second year as the Secretary of State of New Jersey, responsible for arts, history and cultural affairs. While in Atlantic City at the Civil Rights Garden for a Black History Month event, I was made aware of a plaque on the boardwalk honoring the presence of Fannie Lou Hamer at the 1964 Democratic Convention. Immediately, plans were put in place to honor the 40th Anniversary of Mrs. Hamer's impact on behalf of the citizens of Mississippi and the role played by the State of New Jersey. As staff of the Historical Commission began to research the various details, I made a call to a personal friend, Lawrence Guyot, to get his story. Guyot supplied me with what seemed on the surface to be a telephone directory of names and numbers. Knowing the staff would supply all the factual details, I sought to find the human interest story. Making my way through the list supplied and transferring to the staff information for background, I accepted a return call from June Johnson.

Over the phone I could detect in her voice that I was about to get the real story. She immediately began interrogating me on my intentions to honor Mrs. Hamer. I could not answer a question prior to another one being hurled at me. She was not about to be a part of anything that would be business as usual and only include a superficial interpretation of Mrs. Hamer's story. Only after being assured that I was committed to telling Mrs. Hamer's full story would she agree to continue our contacts.

After many conversations with June that took place over two to three months, I learned of the 15 year old girl from Mississippi who was beaten by police at the same time as Fannie Lou Hamer. June Johnson was not telling me the story as a bystander but as an actual participant. Through the memories of her personal physical pain, June told the story of a teen-ager growing up in the South not old enough to vote at the time. June told her story not for a place in history, but for me to understand Fannie Lou Hamer, the person she followed and idolized. June Johnson's passion took the place of the stoic first impressions I had remembered prior to the beginning of our conversations. I recall her telling me of the encounter with her parents when they got to the jail to retrieve her after the beating. Face bloody and bruised with a childish demeanor, but an adult determination not to turn her back on the Movement, she refused to respond when her parents "told" her she could not participate with SNCC. Understanding the penalties for lying to one's parents, June laughed aloud as she told me of the expressions on her parents' faces all the while imagining the punishment she would get once she returned home. Needless to say, June Elizabeth Johnson continued her work with SNCC in helping those she believed were treated unfairly and needed her help.

My favorite story told by June allowed me to see both the confrontational demeanor attributed to her and the passion that I had come to know. She was at the bedside of Mrs. Hamer, if my mental records have not failed. June was 29 years old, 14 years after her beating. Disappointment took hold of her as she tried to manage her anger while being attentive to Mrs. Hamer. She described feelings of anger as she wondered where were all the family and friends that Mrs. Hamer had assisted. Why was Mrs. Hamer without adequate healthcare or an ability to pay her bills? June was attempting to reconcile in her mind the reality before her. Fourteen years had passed and everyone had gone about their business. She recalled stories, told and written, of African American leaders; yet, before her, one of the leading authorities had been forgotten. Her countenance changed as I saw the image of the 15 year old girl appear before me. Tears formed in my eyes as her story continued.

Mrs. Hamer was sweating and June looked for a cloth to wipe her face, but found none. Mrs. Hamer told her to sit while she reached in her gown for a sock that she was using as a kind of breast prosthesis. June laughed as she recalled how Mrs. Hamer laughed at herself and began to listen as June updated her on all the local gossip.

Lawrence Guyot, a member of SNCC, played an important role in the 1964 "Freedom Summer Project" in Mississippi and has continued to participate actively in defending the rights of others. Lawrence Guyot is a graduate of Tougaloo College in Tougaloo, Mississippi and Rutgers University Law School in Newark, New Jersey.

Mr. Guyot presents his memories of June Johnson in the context of her birthplace, Greenwood, Mississippi, her affiliation with SNCC and the involvement of the Department of Justice in the civil rights movement in Mississippi. He declares that June Johnson was involved in all aspects of the movement in Greenwood, through her affiliation with a number of civil rights organizations, including SNCC, COFO, MFDP, NAACP and SCLC.

June Johnson knew from personal experience the price to be paid for freedom. En route home following a week long SCLC Citizenship School Program held in Charleston, South Carolina, she and several others were arrested and sent to the Winona, Mississippi jail. It was there that she experienced the trauma of physical brutality which would leave lifelong scars. It was during this time that she witnessed the suffering of Fannie Lou Hamer, who had been severely beaten in the jail and learned of the killing of Medgar Evers. It was in 1963 that June Johnson committed herself to the civil rights movement and declared "I don't care what happens to me—I'm going to be free or continue to be part of a struggle to fight for the freedom of people in this country. I've done nothing else in my life and I intend to do that for the rest of my life."

June was not an observer but an active participant in the planning and implementation of the actions that occurred in the civil rights movement. She helped black citizens register to vote in Greenwood, the perfect location for her efforts. The scope and degree of terror directed at the potential voters and those working in the Voting Rights Campaign manifested in arrests, shootings, burnings, the curtailment of public food distribution and threats to those who received Social Security payments. The Department of Justice was forced to go to court to stop the violence.

June worked very hard during the civil rights movement and participated in a number of marches designed to call attention to the plight of black citizens in the South. She was involved in the March on Washington in 1963, the march from Selma to Montgomery, Alabama and the James Meredith March. She worked with Robert Kennedy and Marian Wright Edelman to support the funding of the Child Development Group of Mississippi. She also worked to fund the North Mississippi Rural Legal Services. Her efforts were widespread, intensive and continuous.

June Johnson relocated to Washington, D.C., in 1983, continuing her work for the community in the Office of Early Childhood Development. In the District of Columbia she became a member of the State Executive Committee and was elected a delegate from the District to the 2004 Democratic Party Convention. June received her bachelor of arts degree in sociology from Stillman College in Tuscalusa, Alabama, and her master of science degree in education (guidance and counseling) from Jackson State University. Her community efforts and her educational achievements led to a number of speaking engagements to aid the movement. She spoke at the Symposium for Mississippi Freedom Fighters in February, 2006 at Mississippi Valley State College. She emphasized that several events occurred in her life that challenged her to work for civil rights in the United States. Among those events she noted was the killing of Emmett Till, the recollection of her mother being spat upon and her brother being challenged in his yard at home.

June helped black citizens register to vote in LeFlore County. Her efforts in Greenwood, Mississippi led to the development of more local leadership than any other project or any other organization working in the South. June Johnson learned that by being involved with the community and the various civil rights organizations that she could fight the state of Mississippi, she could fight the Sovereignty Commission, the

Citizens Council and the Klan and challenge the indifference of people in the United States—she could do that on her terms and at her pace. June learned that she could do what Bob Moses and Stokely Carmichael learned; i.e., she could change the political climate in Greenwood as empowerment is both transformative and contagious.

June not only changed her life but she affected positively the lives of most people to whom she was exposed. She was empowered by strong people and strong ideas and in turn she empowered others. June said she wanted to see a black woman elected governor of Mississippi. She wanted people to say about her that she was one who always fought for civil rights regardless of the odds.

June and I worked together in Washington, D.C., in the Department of Human Services. We shared information and strategies from 1962 until her death in 2007. I spoke at her funeral because I knew that she would have spoken at mine. I sat with the packed church gathering in order to celebrate her life and declared to those present that if there is anyone here who had not argued with her they should raise their hand in order to be escorted out of the church for their own protection. After the laughter subsided, I said that June had worked to bring about change on her own terms. She gave no favor and sought none. I feel privileged to have been able to watch June Johnson grow and mature.

June was kind, giving to others, especially her family and she understood the importance of treating people with dignity and integrity. She was compassionate and caring and, at the same time, totally committed to empowering people so they could transform the world as they knew it. June will always be missed.

Annie Devine

"America, you got to think about your soul."

Annie Devine was one of the founders and leaders of the Mississippi Freedom Democratic Party (MFDP). She was described by Victoria Gray Adams as the "Wisdom of the Movement." She was one of three African American women, including Victoria Gray Adams and Fannie Lou Hamer, to be seated in the House of Representatives in Washington, D.C., in the late 1960's.

The Reverend Barbara Devine Russell

Many historical treatises document the importance of Annie Devine in the civil rights movement. This chapter, written by her daughter, Barbara, with contributions by her son, Andrew, and grandson, Caleb, is unique in bringing Annie Devine to the reader as a mother, grandmother, friend and human being. Her Christian values are emphasized by her daughter, a Christian minister, as extremely influential in her life and in her decision to help others.

I never considered my mother the average homemaker. She was pious and professional, always striving for a better life for herself and her children. A woman of great strength and faith, she loved people, especially children, and the children loved her. She was a teacher from her heart and also remained teachable until death.

My mother, Annie Devine, was born in 1911 in Mobile, Alabama. When she was three years of age, her parents separated and she was sent to Mississippi to be cared for by her grandmother, who died when Annie was 12. At that time, she went to live with her Aunt Sallie Sherrod, who became known as "Big Mama."

From the time I can remember, Ma was never a very domesticated woman. I don't know how we learned to cook, clean and dress ourselves. Either it came naturally or we learned it by observation. When we were young, Daddy did all the cooking, and as we got older, my brother Andrew and I assumed responsibility for the kitchen. Our home was always clean and pleasant, never cluttered, free from all irritating animals and insects except for a few mice at one time. We drank lots of milk, ate lots of oatmeal and rice, peanut butter crackers and cheese. Sunday meals always consisted of pot roast with potatoes, carrots and onions. We always had carrots on the table. We always had lots of child craft and nursery rhyme books to read. Ma was very conscious of nutrition so we didn't eat a lot of highly seasoned food.

We didn't have lots of clothes, but Ma always bought the best. I remember how she struggled to buy my sister Monet the navy blue dress with the light blue chiffon scarf for the Glee Club school choir. It was also a struggle for Ma to purchase a clarinet for Monet to be in the school band and even more of a struggle to purchase reeds for the clarinet, but Ma did. Alex got his B-B gun and Junior got his train set. I got my paper dolls. When it was my turn to be in a beauty contest, my dress was the most beautiful one. I won the local competition, but lost at state.

We all started out in the Catholic school because it was known to be the best school to get a good early childhood education. We never thought we were poor, even though between the new pairs of Buster Brown's we wore shoes with the heel coming off; still I never felt I was poor. I always felt special and favored.

Ma was a kindhearted, soft spoken person, one who encouraged her children to be the best that they could be. She never kicked you when you were down. On the contrary, Mama's best qualities came out when you were "down." She was there for you and not once do I remember her telling me, "I told you so," even though she was always "telling us so." You could say she "preached" to us all the time. That was her method of training and discipline. It was just too hard for Ma to try to whip us. She would call all the children to hold the one down she was trying to whip. But the one on top would get all the licks, so Ma tried another tactic and that was—the preach/index—finger method. She had an index finger that she would point at you "while preaching" to you, and you just wanted her to go on and give you a good beating. My friend's parents would call them names and curse them out. I wanted Mama to do the same to me, but instead, I got the finger which was much worse, in my opinion.

Mama didn't have any pet sayings that I can remember; she would just talk in general about whatever the matter was at the time. Mostly, she talked about what to do and what not to do and what would happen if you did what you were not to do. Maybe I got this conversation because I was different from my brothers and sister. I was headstrong and stubborn, and very rebellious. I was a very hard child to raise, so Mama's tactic was to constantly warn me of my impending destruction with the finger pointed. I regret today, that I didn't listen to Mama. I'm sure my life would have been different in a positive way. I never really knew or appreciated Mama's wisdom. Others would ask me with incredulous surprise, "But Barbara, can't you see it! (speaking of Ma's wisdom and discernment).

Two sayings of Ma's: "If you make your bed hard, you got to sleep in it" and "you've got to pay the piper," referring to suffering the consequences for one's actions. And for me, also, the constant admonition was, ""Barbara Nell, you've got to be humble." I saw being humble then different from the way I understand it now.

An excerpt from a letter Ma wrote to my sister Monet in September 1973:

I'm so concerned that my children, Monet, Junior, Barbara and Alex, all of whom I feel are the sweetest and loveliest brood in the whole world, do not feel toward each other as I feel toward them. I do feel that you all deserve to make your own way in life and will overcome the odds whatever they be. There will be mistakes, but if we are wise, we will profit by them. It so happens that mama has only one thing to pass on to you to help you in this battle of life and that is this: "Trust the Lord always and seek to do His will."

Ma's whole life revolved around her church, her job and her family. We didn't see Ma much because mostly she worked long hours in the day. We attended Bible Study every Wednesday night at St. Paul AME Zion Church at 505 South Union Street in Canton. Ma's life-long membership was at St. Paul except for the time she spent in Michigan and Nebraska. She always took us to church. In addition to Bible School, we attended Varrick Christian Endeavor on Sunday evenings, prayer meetings, Sunday School every Sunday and all the revivals, conferences and programs. Ma was faithful to her church and always fulfilled her assignment be it large or small. She was fondly called Ms. "D," or "Mama D," and was very active, dearly beloved, and respected by the church members. Her counsel and wisdom was sought in her church and community until her death. Reverend Richmond, one of the former pastors of St. Paul, always stayed at Ma's house when he was in town on church business.

This was the church Aunt Sallie Sherrod took her to at a very young age and wouldn't allow her to sit anywhere but on the front seat. No back seat for Annie. It is Ma's joy in serving in the church that remains in my memory. As a child, I watched her in the choir processional during Sunday morning worship.

Ma utilized her spiritual gifts in the church serving diligently as church secretary for many years, president of the Senior Choir, Superintendent of Church Sunday School, Director of Christian Education, Sunday School Teacher and member of the Board of Trustees. One Christmas Ma taught us a Christmas play and we performed it. I remember one occasion I was in an oratorical contest during one of our church conferences. It was obvious to everyone that I won the contest, but the judges awarded the prize to another child. Ma was so angry, she was about to start a commotion; I had to calm her down and tell her it didn't matter. She was always a fighter for what she thought was right.

During her time as Senior Choir Director, we got a new pastor. His wife was a musician and not a very good one. The pastor wanted his wife to play for the Senior Choir, but Ma didn't want her to because they liked the musician they had. Needless to say, the pastor was not very pleased and moved to replace Ma soon thereafter. This will give you insight into Ma's character; she was impartial in most things and sought excellence in whatever the endeavor. Her attitude was that way with family, friend or foe.

Ma also sought truthfulness and honesty in her life and she taught us to be honest and respectful. One time I stole an apple from Mr. George Washington's grocery store and hadn't quite eaten it all up by the time I made it home. Ma wanted to know where I got the apple. I couldn't think of an immediate answer and she surmised I had gotten it by questionable means. I confessed I "took" it from Mr. Washington's store. Ma made me take the apple back and "tell" Mr. Washington I stole it. I did exactly what she told me to do. Since then I have the proclivity to obey rules to the letter, which sometimes gets me in trouble. The only real whipping I ever got was for making fun of an elderly lady who was our neighbor. I learned not only to respect my elders, but to care deeply for them.

When Ma was a little girl her Aunt Sallie Sherrod enjoyed having Annie read to her. Ma couldn't read but she pretended she could. She would look at the pictures in a book and make up a story. When Aunt Sallie Sherrod discovered Ma was making up the stories and couldn't read at all, she went on a mission to teach Annie to read, and Annie became the best reader in her class. Ma liked to say that she enjoyed reading and spelling but not arithmetic, "It was too much to think about."

Ma was a member of the first twelfth grade graduating class from Cameron Street High School. Up 'til then, the eighth grade was the graduating level. Ma was supposed to have been the valedictorian of her class, but because of her skin color (Ma was very dark skinned), a student "brighter" (light skinned, with "good" hair) was selected to be valedictorian. Ma graduated salutatorian.

Aunt Sallie Sherrod did domestic work all day and then took in washing and ironing in her home at night to help make ends meet. Ma would have to go pick up the clothes from Aunt Sallie's customers and bring them to the house. Ma was very indignant about having to tote clothes across town; this task was truly beneath Ma's dignity.

Finally, Ma decided to go back to school. She began teaching school at Burgess High School in Flora, Mississippi. The person who influenced her the most was Velma Ware Jackson, a teacher and district supervisor of schools. She was tall, dark and beautiful with long hair and a dynamite shape. A very educated and smart woman, she was Ma's inspiration. While attending Tougaloo Southern Christian College, Ma didn't make the grade she thought she deserved on one of her papers. During a conference with her instructor about this matter, she was told to be sure to "dot all her 'I's and cross all her 'T's." Ma never forgot this lesson.

In the early '50s we moved from Hickory Alley to the projects, the Joe Prichard Homes, which was the first government financed public housing in Canton. The rent was $1.63 a month. Rain, shine, sleet or snow, every month black people, tenants in the projects, would stand outside in long lines to wait their turn to pay their rent. Ma never stood in line. But the time came when the rent was raised. Ours went up to about $2.50 a month. Ma was indignant and informed management that rent was too high and people were not able to pay. When she did not get a satisfactory answer, she wrote a letter to HUD stating that this rent increase was creating a hardship not only on her but on all the tenants. Well, we got a letter stating the rent would not be raised for any of the tenants, but would remain the same. I believe the rent at the Joe Prichard Homes remained stable for a long time. This was Ma's second act of social activism.

It was hard for Ma to get to her job at Burgess High School (since Flora was about 20 miles West of Canton), so Ma decided to seek employment elsewhere. First she sold handiwipes and made enough to pay the bills. Then she got a job with Security Life Insurance Company, a black owned and operated insurance company. Ma didn't need a car. She walked the streets and knocked on doors and sold insurance. She loved her job. Her idol was Mr. Snodgrass, top salesman on the staff. Ma set out to be the number one top salesperson at Security. She knew this was her ticket out of poverty and now we were going to be rich. This work experience was good training for the work that she would later do in Voter Registration/Education and the organization of MFDP.

For the first time I could remember, we had a brand new living room set, a beautiful couch and love seat and matching lamps and tables. Needless to say, the dream of wealth never materialized. Along came the civil rights movement and Ma was drafted by Ann Moody–the rest is history.

In Old South, Ma would have been called an "uppity nigger" because she was not humble enough to submit to the standards of relationship customarily displayed between blacks and whites. Ma refused to use the term "yassum or yassuh" like most black people did when responding to whites in conversation. Instead, Ma answered, "well," which did not gain her any favor with any white folks. Word got around when black people did not conform to expectations.

From an early age, Ma was aware of the difference in the way blacks were treated as opposed to whites. Black women only worked in the homes of white women. She wanted to know why blacks and whites were not together. She recalled always using old textbooks in school that had been discarded by the white students. Even at the age of eight, she was aware that people seemed more separate, and she wanted to know why. She recalled that she had asked at an early age: "What can we black folks do besides chop cotton?"

Ma's attitude could have come from her background. While typically blacks did not own land, both her paternal and maternal grandparents were landowners. Her grandpa, on her mother's side, owned 300 acres of land which he left as an inheritance for his children. Ma's grandma, on her father's side of the family, was also a landowner and never a share-cropper. They left the land to their children and grandchildren. Ma never lived on the land with the other members of the family, except when she was very young; she always lived in town with Aunt Sallie Sherrod. One cold Saturday, when times were hard, Ma took all four of her children, and caught a cotton truck from the projects and went to the cotton field. It was so cold, we made a fire. Between all five of us, I doubt we picked 50 pounds of cotton. That must have been a really bad time for Ma. I don't remember ever being hungry, neither do I remember ever having our lights or gas turned off. One time, when Ma was broke and had no money, her brother, Uncle Garfield, who lived in Detroit, sent her $5.00 in the mail.

I never heard Ma complain about money or anything else. I do remember her coming home during the time she sold handiwipes. She would have worked all day until late at night. Her feet would be so tired. She would always wake me up and tell me to cook her something to eat. We must have been doing fairly well at that time because she always told me to cook her a steak with gravy and rice. I usually complained but got up and cooked Ma what she wanted. She never asked Monet or Andrew, who were older than I—it was always me.

Annie's son, Andrew, does not recall his mother taking government commodities such as cheese, rice or beans. He does recall Annie encouraging her children to become educated. Andrew thought college for him was unlikely because of lack of funds, but he knew there was never a question that if he graduated from high school he would go.

Andrew also noted that Annie was "incredibly religious." Her life revolved around her church and her work. She spent most of her time reading the Bible. Andrew made a point to explain that Annie never read aloud from the Bible. She was not outspoken about her faith and did not push her beliefs on her children. Andrew states that his mother did not have any vices such as alcohol, gambling or drugs. She once told Andrew about a reception she attended in Washington, D.C., where she accidentally picked up a glass of champagne. She did not know what to do with the glass, so she carried it around with her the rest of the evening without ever drinking any of the champagne.

Other qualities that Annie had, according to Andrew, were taking herself seriously and never gossiping about others. She told Andrew a story about a protest she was in that was broken up by the police. Instead of putting the protesters in jail, the police put them all into a fenced off area and no charges were pressed. Andrew would joke with his mother that he would tell her grandchildren that she was a convict. Andrew said mother became very indignant, and he had to apologize. Andrew does not remember a time when Annie Devine was not the strongest person in the room. According to Andrew, "She kept herself neat; she was practical and never wanted expensive items." He said she was content with her life.

Excerpts from a letter sent to her daughter, Monet, on November 29, 1974:

> *There have been so many times in my life when burdens pressed down so hard on me and I had to face them alone but I kept my trust in my Heavenly Father and He unfolded to me day by day what to do. He kept back the people and things that could have destroyed me. That involved everything I was connected with, even my husband.*

Ma's mother's name was Rosa Carson and her daddy was Author Robinson, whom she never knew. She knew her step-dad, Garfield Heath. Ma never talked about life with her mother. Her grandson, Caleb, recalls asking her which generation she was in, and she explained concisely that she was in the "Robinson generation." (Presumably, she meant Jackie Robinson, the first African American major league baseball player.)

The only one she talked about was Aunt Sallie Sherrod, who raised her. Aunt Sallie Sherrod gave up her life with her husband, the Reverend Alex Sherrod, to care for her ailing mother, Grandma Easter. Aunt Sallie

Sherrod also looked after her brother, Uncle Tunk. Her home was also used as a boarding house for young girls who lived in the country but attended school in town. She kept many young girls in her home. Some paid her, but most didn't. According to Ma, Aunt Sallie was very good to them. She fed them, bought them clothes and took good care of them. One of the ladies who lived with Aunt Sallie Sherrod never forgot her kindness, and expressed her appreciation by keeping up Ma's burial insurance until she passed.

Clearly, Aunt Sallie Sherrod was the most dominant influence in Ma's life. She raised Ma from a little child and modeled a life of Christian values through her lifestyle and service to others. She instilled in her a work ethic and compassion and concern for others stemming from a love of God and love of neighbor as oneself. Aunt Sallie Sherrod was married to Reverend Alex Sherrod who was assigned to a church out of state, but Aunt Sallie could not leave her ailing mother to accompany her husband, so they separated. Ma believed Aunt Sallie Sherrod to be the strongest person she ever knew, especially her work ethic and her sacrificial life for her family and for those girls who needed her. Aunt Sallie Sherrod used to dip snuff. When she decided to quit, she put the snuff box on the dresser and never picked it up again.

Ma didn't set out to become a well known civil rights activist. She followed the path that was set for her life. And I believe her upbringing and Christian training prepared her for the work she was to do in the civil rights movement. In her work, Annie Devine was called the "Wise Elder"; Fannie Lou Hamer was the "spokesperson" and Vicky (Victoria Gray Adams) was the "Kid." During the summer of 1964, Vicky was a regular at our apartment at 347-D Jo Prichard Homes, Canton, Mississippi. I do remember seeing Ms. Hamer at our apartment one time. Ma told a friend, Fannie Lou "could talk you off your seat if you let her." In September I went to college at Tougaloo and might have missed Ms. Hamer's more frequent visits.

When Ma heard that the civil rights movement was moving south and was upon us, she moved to organize the Madison County movement, which gave the national movement an organization to plug into when the movement finally got to Canton. Ma's attitude was that "they did not want outsiders taking credit for our movement." She got together six other people besides herself, all men, and they organized the Madison County Movement. An annual prayer breakfast is held in memory of these brave people, with the purpose of identifying and fostering servant leaders. The prayer breakfast has inspired ministries, and young people to get involved in politics and community service. I believe that the Spirit of Sallie Sherrod and Annie Devine is with them.

Annie became involved in the civil rights movement in the early 1960s. Her daughter, Monet, worried about Annie and the work she was doing because she knew how dangerous it was. Not only was there a danger of physical harm, but economic instability and uncertainty for those who challenged the status quo. Monet had jobs in the movement also, but her jobs were not as dangerous as her mother's.

Annie, Fannie Lou and Victoria were three fearless, dedicated and courageous women. They traveled many miles to organize the Mississippi Freedom Democratic Party. They held meetings in the brush harbors and in churches and on farms, traveling to country towns day and night. They organized the MFDP, which would be the vehicle to run political candidates on the Freedom ticket because they were not allowed to participate in the regular Democratic Party election process. Without the MFDP, the black people would not have been able to run for political office and the movement would have been ineffective as far as gaining influence and power. It would have been like a seed planted in the ground whose roots and stems spring forth, but never blossoms into a flower.

Annie Devine described attending the MFDP Convention for the Democratic Party in 1964 in Atlantic City, as extremely exciting: "Like her favorite foods, collard greens, hamhocks and apple sauce." She said, "It was brand new, there was nothing like it before or since." She was especially taken with the idea of grass roots groups of people organizing against the establishment, a group of excited people coming together to work toward a common purpose. She said, "It made Atlantic City an important city at that time," and commented on the lack of violence demonstrated during this critical period.

Her son, Andrew, described Annie as not interested in going public with any of the experiences that she had during the civil rights movement. She did not want to profit from the work she did. The problems of racism were only raised in practical discussions about avoiding dangerous places or situations.

Andrew left home for the military at the beginning of the civil rights movement. He was with his mother when Annie delivered her first list of registered voters to the courthouse in Canton, Mississippi.

Later in life, Annie's grandchildren became very important to her. After the civil rights movement, Annie's health began to fail. She had heart disease most of her life. Her heart problems were serious, but she tried not to let her illness affect her work.

Annie moved to Omaha, Nebraska, where Andrew lived. She moved there because of health problems, including heart disease. Before Omaha, Annie had lived in Canton, Mississippi, where Andrew felt she was not getting the health care she needed. The time she spent with Andrew in Nebraska was one of the longest periods of time they had spent together and was memorable for both. Although she was enjoying living with Andrew in Nebraska, Annie missed her church and her home in Mississippi. She felt it was necessary to return to Mississippi when she learned of an emerging political crisis within her church.

Although she loved living with all of her children and grandchildren, her heart was in Canton with her church. Following her return, her health worsened and she "withered away" until she died.

My conclusion is that God's word was manifested in Ma's life, as she learned it, believed it, loved it, obeyed it to the best of her ability and claimed it for her own. She followed the path that was meant for her to follow. The significance of Annie Devine's role in the civil rights movement was the articulation of the needs not only of Mississippians, but the universal needs of poor people who had been previously overlooked and intentionally left out.

Joan Sadoff (editor) and Ellen Spendrup (cousin of Florence Mars)

Victoria Gray Adams and Flonzie Brown-Wright, "Standing on My Sisters' Shoulders"

Constance Slaughter-Harvey

June Elizabeth Johnson

Gloria Dickerson

Unita Blackwell

Victoria Gray Adams, Dorrie Ladner and Flonzie Brown-Wright, "Standing on My Sisters' Shoulders"

Joan Mulholland

Joan Sadoff, Producer, "Standing on My Sisters' Shoulders"
Laura Lipson, Director, "Standing on My Sisters' Shoulders" and Virginia Gray Adams
Kennedy Center, Washington, DC, October 1, 2004

Gravestone of Fannie Lou Hamer

Betty Pearson

Mae Bertha Carter

Winson Hudson

Group picture: "Standing on My Sisters' Shoulders"—Winifred Green, Gloria Dickerson, Flonzie Brown-Wright, L.C. Dorsey, Dorrie Ladner, Betty Pearson, June Elizabeth Johnson, Constance Slaughter-Harvey, Joan Mulholland, Victoria Gray Adams. (The one male in the picture, between Joan Mulholland and Victoria Gray Adams, is Charlie Cobb, organizer for the Student Non-violent Coordinating Committee (SNCC).)

Fannie Lou Hamer

"The only thing they could do was kill me, and
it seemed like they'd been trying to do that a little
bit at a time ever since I could remember."

Fannie Lou Hamer led with her voice—singing and speaking as she confronted the inequities of racism with determination and extraordinary courage. Her voice resonated with urgency as she demanded, "The right to live like other human beings in America." Her leadership in the civil rights movement is legendary.

Monica Land, Grandniece of Fannie Lou Hamer

Monica Land, originally from Chicago, has been a writer for more than 20 years. She is an award winning author with extensive research in black history. She has produced several television biographies on Dorothy Dandridge and interviewed numerous civil rights figures, including Rosa Parks, Mamie Till-Mobley (mother of Emmet Till), Myrlie Evers (widow of MedgarEvers, black civil rights leader), and James Meredith.

All my life, I had heard my family speak of this mythic figure: a woman who not only prayed for change, but vowed herself to bring it. They laughed when they recalled the funny things she said or did, but their faces turned somber, cold and sad when they remembered the pain and suffering she endured. I knew she was a relative, and I even remember seeing her once or twice, but the full scope of who and what she was would remain unknown to me for many years. What added to the mystique of Aunt Fannie Lou was that we have almost no pictures of her. And the ones we do have are old black and whites. I often wondered what she was thinking as she sat there perfectly poised, still and quiet.

Who was Fannie Lou Hamer?

To me, and most of my family, she was an aunt. She married my grandfather's brother in the 1940s, and they lived together in Sunflower Country, Mississippi. My family speaks of her fondly as a woman who loved to laugh and sing and worked hard for everything she ever had. They said she had such an electrifying personality, that she could "light up a room" simply by walking into it. To the rest of the world, however, Aunt Fannie Lou was a woman who was "sick and tired of being sick and tired." Again I wonder if most people really knew what she was "sick and tired of?"

Aunt Fannie Lou spent most of her years in rural southern poverty, entering politics and the civil rights movement in spite of her limited sixth grade education. Aunt Fannie Lou worked endlessly and tirelessly, late in her life, for political, social, and economic reform, not only for herself, but for all Americans, black and white. She was considered by far one of the most eloquent speakers of the civil rights movement.

Born on a plantation in Montgomery County, Mississippi, on October 6, 1917, Aunt Fannie Lou was the granddaughter of slaves and the youngest of 20, having 14 brothers and five sisters. Her parents, Jim and Lou Ella

Townsend, were sharecroppers who had to feed their entire family on $1.25 per day. Times were extremely hard for the Townsend family; they lived in constant need, often lacking sufficient food, clothing, shelter and medicine. As a child, Aunt Fannie Lou contracted polio and suffered greatly due to the lack of a vaccine. Many say the polio was the cause of her pronounced limp while others said it was because her brother dropped her as a child. Regardless of the cause, Aunt Fannie Lou never allowed her physical disability to hinder her in any way.

When Aunt Fannie Lou was 2-years old, her family moved to Sunflower County, Mississippi, to a plantation owned by E. W. Brandon. Aunt Fannie Lou lived on this plantation until she was an adult and admitted that life under Brandon was "very hard," because the family never had enough to eat. At that time, the school year for the black children lasted about four months, when they were not mandated to pick or chop cotton in the fields. Aunt Fannie Lou was forced to quit school when she was in the sixth-grade because of her family's constant workload and the lack of adequate clothing. In fact, they often wore sacks tied around their feet for lack of shoes. In spite of that, Aunt Fannie Lou had an insatiable thirst for knowledge and read everything she could find.

"I worked in the fields," she once said. "In fact, all the kids in the Delta worked in the fields. Wasn't no other work to do. They didn't have any factories; wasn't nothing to do but field work. And when there was no cotton to chop, we would be raking corn stalks or doing something like [that] . . ."

When she was six years of age, she reported that she was "tricked into a life of servitude" by the plantation owner. "I was playing beside the road," Aunt Fannie Lou once said, "and this plantation owner drove up to me and asked me could I pick cotton. I told him I didn't know how, and he said 'Yes you can.'" Thus, with the promise of gingerbread cookies, sardines and Cracker Jacks from his commissary store, the plantation owner, Mr. Brandon, coaxed Aunt Fannie Lou Hamer into a life of hard labor. She said, "I picked 30 pounds of cotton that week. But I found out that he was trapping me into continuing the work that I was to keep doing." Indeed, it was a trap, because the landowners gave store credit to all the plantation workers in order to buy supplies they needed to grow cotton.

However, the prices they charged, were so excessive, the workers stayed in debt and were therefore unable to leave the plantation.

Aunt Fannie Lou Hamer also remained in Brandon's debt picking 60 pounds of cotton the second week, and by the age of 13, she was picking 200 to 300 pounds per week. With such a large family, the Townsends could easily grow and produce more than 37,000 pounds of cotton each year, but more often than not, at the end of each year, when the accounts were totaled, sharecroppers, like the Townsends, usually owed the landowners money rather than earning any for themselves. The lack of an education was also a factor in this never ending cycle. Many sharecroppers couldn't read or write, and therefore, couldn't keep sufficient records of what they borrowed and what was owed.

Aunt Fannie Lou had a similar experience as a child when one year her family produced sufficient crops to rent their own land, fix up their little house, buy some mules and purchase a tractor. For the first time, Aunt Fannie Lou said they could see the light of hope.

"We were doing pretty well, she said. "My father bought a car. And one night, this white man went to our lot where the mules were eating, and stirred up a gallon of Paris Green [arsenic insecticide] into the mule's food. It killed everything we had. The poisoning knocked us right back down flat. We never did get back up again. That white man did it just because we were getting somewhere. White people never liked to see Negroes get a little success."

Aunt Fannie Lou was often discouraged, and she admitted that at times she "wished [she] was white." But her mother, Ms. Lou Ella Townsend, taught Aunt Fannie Lou to always be proud of who she was and where she came from. Even so, her life as a sharecropper still made her angry. Eventually, Aunt Fannie Lou vowed to do something for black people in the South, even if it meant her death.

After they were married, Uncle Pap and Aunt Fannie Lou moved to the Marlow Plantation, in Ruleville, Mississippi, where they lived and worked as sharecroppers. They never had any children of their own because, without her knowledge or consent, Aunt Fannie Lou, like so many other black women of that time, had been sterilized during a visit to the doctor. Some time later, Aunt Fannie Lou and Uncle Pap adopted and raised two young girls whose families were financially unable to care for them. While they worked on the plantation, though, Uncle Pap and Aunt Fannie Lou continued to witness the gross mistreatment of the black workers firsthand. Aunt Fannie Lou told the following account of what happened while she was there. "When I was cleaning the boss' house, his daughter came up to me and said, 'You don't have to clean this (room) too good . . . it's just old Honey's.' Old Honey was the dog. I just couldn't get over the dog having a bathroom when the owner wouldn't even have the toilet fixed for us." Aunt Fannie Lou concluded, "Negroes in Mississippi were treated worse than dogs." As they labored on the plantation, Aunt Fannie Lou's concern for her people intensified, but she inwardly struggled for an effective way to help them.

Usually on the weekends, Aunt Fannie Lou and Uncle Pap would often visit her family in Kilmichael, Mississippi and they would spend time with my mother's family or another of Uncle Pap's brothers, L. B., and his wife, Getha. Despite the harsh treatment they endured on the plantation, my mother's oldest brother, Jim, still remembers the Aunt Fannie Lou who found the strength to laugh. He states: "I was about 11 or 12 when they came to visit daddy, They would sit around and eat and drink and have a good time and Aunt Fannie Lou would joke a lot. She talked about other things as well, but the funny stories are what really stuck with me. She told one story in particular about a Banty Rooster and a man who had some chickens. Every time she came out to visit, my mother would ask her to tell that story. No one could tell stories like Aunt Fannie Lou."

In those times, telling stories, singing church songs, playing cards, and eating were the social activities of the day. In fact, the kitchen was probably the most sacred room in the house. "Aunt Fannie Lou would always go right into the kitchen when she came to our house, and ask mama, 'What can I do for you?'" Jim said.

Other family members agreed that Aunt Fannie Lou was a hard worker who always had a lively and optimistic demeanor. And despite the adversity and obstacles she faced, she was determined to change her situation and that of others. "She was tired of the life she was living and her health wasn't always good," my cousin, Minnie (Hamer) Hoskins, said. "That's what she was 'sick and tired' of. And long before she was involved in politics or the civil rights movement she would always say that she was 'sick and tired of being sick and tired.' She and my uncle didn't have much. They had to borrow money during the winter and then they worked all summer and she said they would never get ahead. But she was still a fun person to be around and she just decided that someday she was going to do better."

Minnie, whose parents were Uncle L.B. and Aunt Getha, also said that Aunt Fannie Lou taught her the value of prayer and would often attend church with the family at Shady Grove Methodist in Kilmichael. "I asked her once," Minnie said, "How do you know what to say when you get down on your knees? And Aunt Fannie Lou said, 'Just fall on your knees and say, 'Our Father,' and he will put the words in your mouth.'"

Minnie's brother, James W. Hamer, agreed that Aunt Frannie Lou was a woman of great faith and would often relate stories from the Bible and sing church hymns. "She was a great singer," James said. "She would come to our church at Shady Grove . . . and she would always sing, 'This Little Light of Mine.'"

James believed that Aunt Fannie Lou's natural skill as a speaker was a God-given ability and was especially apparent when she spoke before the congregants at church. "She was tenacious and steadfast in whatever she did, and she did it to the fullest of her ability," he said. "Even when she was picking cotton, she wanted to pick more cotton than anyone else. Aunt Fannie Lou absolutely influenced my life. I was born and reared in Mississippi and my mom and dad taught us to revere white people. If they said something negative to us, we were just to take it and go away. But after seeing what Aunt Fannie Lou did and how she lived her life, seeing what she went through to get people to register to vote, I said, 'If she can do it, I can do it.' And from that point on, I never backed down from any situation, especially as it pertained to being black and trying to get ahead."

Minnie felt similarly about Aunt Fannie Lou and her influence on her identity as a black woman. She described how dangerous life was for black people in the South during the 1950s and 1960s. "Emmett Till and a lot of other people had gotten killed," Minnie said. "And mama always told us to be careful of what you said and what you did. But Aunt Fannie Lou impacted my life by opening my eyes to things that I wasn't aware of."

My mother also said that Aunt Fannie Lou's influence on her life was significant. "I knew the only way we were going to accomplish anything in Mississippi was to get away from there and that's what I did. She helped me to see that if you wanted anything in life, you had to put it in your mind and in your heart to accomplish it. That was a valuable lesson for me when I left Mississippi."

Listening to my relatives talk about Aunt Fannie Lou helped me to understand who she really was. Through their eyes I saw her as a caring, charming and strong black woman who, even with the difficulties in her life, refused to let it affect her inner spirit. Still, Aunt Fannie Lou wanted and needed to do something to improve the plight of black people living in the South. Her opportunity surfaced when in 1962, members of the Student Non-Violent Coordinating Committee (SNCC) and the Southern Christian Leadership Conference (SCLC) held a voter registration meeting at her church. Aunt Fannie Lou realized what had to be done. She said earlier: "I didn't know anything about voting. I didn't know anything about registering to vote. I went to the church and they talked about how it was our right to vote. They were talking about the fact that we could vote people out of office that we did not want and that we thought were not doing right by black people. That sounded interesting enough to me that I wanted to try it."

Aunt Fannie Lou was surprised to learn that even though blacks had the constitutional right to vote, they weren't allowed to do so in Mississippi. When SNCC asked for volunteers to go to the courthouse to register to vote, Aunt Fannie Lou was the first to raise her hand. Realizing how dangerous this behavior was, Aunt Fannie Lou later said, "The only thing they could do was kill me, and it seemed like they've been trying to do that a little bit at a time ever since I could remember."

On August 31, 1962, Aunt Fannie Lou found out how real that threat was when she tried to register to vote. As their bus approached the Circuit

Court Clerk's Office in Indianola, Mississippi, several armed men were waiting for them. "When we arrived, there were people with guns, and just a lot of strange people," she said. "We told the clerk we wanted to register to vote. He told all of us that we would have to get out of there, except two. I was one of the two persons that remained inside with a man named Ernest Davis. We stayed there to take the literacy test." The Registrar gave her the 16th section of the Constitution of Mississippi, and told her to copy it as it was printed in the book, and then to give an interpretation of it. Aunt Fannie Lou later said it was impossible for her to do that. "I tried to give it," she said, "but I didn't even know what it meant, much less to interpret it."

On their return trip home, after being turned away from the clerk's office, the bus was stopped by police, and the driver was formally charged. Former SNCC member Lawrence Guyot was there; he said, "When we were coming back to Ruleville, the bus driver was arrested. The charge was driving a bus that was 'too yellow.' They said it was the wrong color. The driver was stopped and charged, and we raised money out of our own pockets to pay his fine."

Guyot also recalls the first time he saw Fannie Lou Hamer: "I met Mrs. Hamer at the mass meeting she attended. James Bevel was there, myself, and James Foreman, and we talked to people from a religious perspective, doing the work of The Lord and the church by going to register to vote. We asked for volunteers and Mrs. Hamer agreed to go. We left the next day. The group included Mrs. Joe Ford, Fannie Lou Hamer, myself, Charles McLaurin, Hollis Watkins, and 15 other people. We went by bus from Ruleville to Indianola. When we arrived, people were hesitant to get off the bus. They all recognized that it could be dangerous, but when Fannie Lou Hamer began singing, people got off the bus to register. Charles McLaurin recounts that this is the day when he really became a man, when he saw these women stand up and walk right through all those highway patrolmen to go in and attempt to register to vote and then get back on the bus."

Guyot confirms that Aunt Fannie Lou's troubles were just beginning. "Word passed rather quickly about Fannie Lou Hamer's attempt to register to vote and that afternoon she was told that either she take her name off the registration or she would have to leave the plantation." Aunt Fannie Lou told Mr. Marlow that she was not going to take her name off the registration. She told him that she didn't go down there to register for him, "I went down there to register for me," she said. Even though Aunt Fannie Lou was forced to leave that night, the landowner refused to release any of their belongings unless Uncle Pap stayed behind to harvest the crops. From that point on, Aunt Fannie Lou became the victim of continual death threats and attempts to kill her by shooting into her house. Aunt Fannie Lou later said, "My house was so full of holes, it wouldn't hold water."

Living as a fugitive, Aunt Fannie Lou moved in with some friends, Mr. and Mrs. Robert Tucker. And about a week after the move the Tucker's house was shot at 16 times. The shots were meant for Aunt Fannie Lou. Other homes were shot into as well, including the McDonald's and Herman Sissel's, where two female students from Jackson State University were hit, one critically, in the head.

Aunt Fannie Lou then fled Ruleville for her life, but she never gave up her quest for political freedom; and in 1963, after three separate attempts, she finally became a registered voter in the state of Mississippi. "I was determined to become a first-class citizen," she later said. After being unable to vote in the next primary elections, because she didn't have the necessary papers, Aunt Fannie Lou decided to cast her first vote—for herself—in her 1964 run for Congress. She didn't win that election, but what she did was breathe new life into the old cliche, "If at first you don't succeed, try, try again."

During that time, Aunt Fannie Lou also encouraged many others to vote, including members of her own family. "I was about 22-years old and I was a teacher," Minnie said. "And Aunt Fannie Lou came to my father's house and she said to me, 'Black people need to get out and register. You're educated, you need to register, and you need to talk to the other teachers to get them to register to vote.' And I was really afraid because I didn't know what to expect. We still had segregation in Mississippi. But when another teacher, Ms Small, and I were talking about it, we decided to go down and register. Aunt Fannie Lou later told me that we were the first blacks to register to vote in Montgomery County."

Aunt Fannie Lou eventually became a field secretary for SNCC in order to assist other blacks to register to vote. Guyot states, "She was a natural leader. In fact, she had been a leader in the plantation system and recorded the weighing of the cotton. Additionally, I would have to say that Mrs. Hamer believed that everything she did in the civil rights movement was based on her religious beliefs. Her fight against segregation was, in her words, "How can I expect to see the face of Jesus if I allow myself to hate somebody else?'"

Aunt Fannie Lou's belief in what she was doing was severely tested on June 9, 1963, when she and several other SNCC members returned from a voter registration workshop in South Carolina. Their bus stopped in Winona, Mississippi, the seat of Montgomery County, the county of Aunt Fannie Lou's birth. When some of the workers went into the "white only" waiting room, the entire group was arrested, including a 14-year old girl named June Johnson. Aunt Fannie Lou later described the incident as follows: "Four of the people got off the bus to use the washroom and two of the people to use the restaurant. When they were ordered out of the restaurant, I was on the bus, and when I looked out the window and saw they had rushed out, I got off the bus to see what had happened. I then got back on the bus, and as soon as I was seated, I saw they began to get the four people in a highway patrolman's car. I stepped off the bus to see what was happening, and somebody screamed from the car, 'Get that one there.' When I went to get in the car, the man told me I was under arrest, and he kicked me."

Aunt Fannie Lou was taken to the city jail where she was severely beaten. As she noted, "I was placed in a cell with Euvester Simpson. I began to hear the sounds of licks and screams. I asked God to have mercy on these people. It wasn't long before three white men came to my cell, one of whom was a state highway patrolman. He said, 'We're going to make you wish you was dead.' I was carried out of that cell into another cell, where they had two Negro prisoners. The state highway patrolman ordered the first Negro to take the blackjack and beat me. After the first Negro beat me until he was exhausted, the patrolman ordered the second

Negro to take the blackjack, and he began to beat me. I began to work my feet, and the highway patrolman ordered the first Negro who had beat me to sit on my feet to keep me from working my feet. I began to scream when one white man got up and began to beat me in my head and tell me to hush. My dress had worked up high, and he pulled my dress down, and then he pulled my dress back up. They kept telling me, 'you nigger bitch, we're gonna make you wish you were dead.'"

Aunt Fannie Lou was beaten mercilessly. No formal charges were made against her or the others. But what charge could they make that would merit such a beating? Aunt Fannie Lou knew it was the result of her attempting to vote. She later described the impact the beating had on her. "They beat me until I was hard, 'til I couldn't bend my fingers or get up when they told me to. When they finally told me to go to my cell, I couldn't get up. I couldn't bend my knees. Every day of my life I pay with the misery of that beating. That's how I got this blood clot in my eye. The sight's nearly gone now, and my kidney was injured from the blows they gave me on the back."

Aunt Fannie Lou learned that NAACP Field Director Medgar Evers had been murdered the morning of her release from jail. Some said his death was the reason they had not been killed in Winona. For her though, the fight was just beginning.

Still a young child living at home in Kilmichael, Mississippi—about 15 miles from Winona—my mother, Mary, questioned why her aunt had tolerated the pain and suffering she endured. She said, "Aunt Fannie Lou came and stayed with us after the beating because there was a lot of conflict going on where she was living. They didn't want her on the land . . . I was a teenager at the time, and I didn't understand why a person would want to go through all of that. But as I got older, I understood. Aunt Fannie Lou wanted something better for herself and for her people. Being a sharecropper, she lived and witnessed misery, and she saw that registering to vote was the only way out for her and her people, so she took a stand."

Attorneys for SNCC bailed Aunt Fannie Lou and the others out of jail and filed a lawsuit against the Winona Police Department. At trial, all the white people involved in the arrest and the beating were found not guilty. Aunt Fannie Lou became more determined than ever to fight for equal rights in Mississippi. "I was in jail with Mrs. Hamer when she was beaten," Guyot said. "I was beaten. Euvester Simpson was beaten, Charles West was beaten, as were others. I saw that Mrs. Hamer could, and would, withstand terror. She stood committed to what she believed in, and she did not allow the beatings to stop her."

In 1964, Aunt Fannie Lou and SNCC formed the Mississippi Freedom Democratic Party (MFDP). At the Democratic Convention in Atlantic City, Aunt Fannie Lou and the other delegates challenged the party for not addressing the concerns of blacks in Mississippi. In an emotional plea that was televised, Aunt Fannie Lou later addressed the Credentials Committee about the injustice of the all-white Democratic delegation. She reminded them of the real reason behind her beating. "All of this," she said of the beating, "is to become first-class citizens. And if the Freedom Democratic Party is not seated now, I question America. Is this America, the land of the free and the home of the brave, where we have to sleep with our telephones off the hooks because our lives be threatened daily, because we want to live as decent human beings in America?" Her words were heart-wrenching. Guyot later said, "She was the right person at the right time, and her speech in Atlantic City has not only been played and analyzed, but it has had a tremendous political effect in pragmatic terms. Her speech was so effective, that President Lyndon Johnson attempted to stop it." According to Guyot "Lyndon Johnson then stepped up his opposition against the Freedom Democratic Party. In his tapes, the details reveal a lot about how he viewed the impact of what the party was doing. Johnson said to the people, 'We cannot have a floor fight on this, because we can't allow the country to see us fighting to seat an all-white delegation in Mississippi and then go back and ask the people of Illinois, California, and New York to vote for us in November.'"

At the time of the Democratic Convention, the only three networks were ABC, CBS, and NBC and each of them played Aunt Fannie Lou's speech in its entirety. Telegrams began to pour in favoring the Freedom Democratic Party. A compromise was reached: Two seats were offered with no voting privileges and a promise that never again would there be an all white delegation. Aunt Fannie refused. "There was a meeting with Hubert Humphrey, Bob Moses and others," Guyot said, "but it was really a subterfuge, because while they were meeting, the MFDP delegates were voting to accept the compromise." Two members of the MFDP, Aaron Henry and Ed King, wanted to go out to the press at the convention hall and say that they would accept the two seat compromise. Aunt Fannie Lou's rejection of the token seats was so strong, that she reportedly told Henry: "You better stay in that convention hall the balance of your life, 'cause if you come out, I'm going to cut your throat." According to Guyot, all the major civil rights leaders tried to persuade Aunt Fannie Lou to accept the compromise. Roy Wilkins, the head of the NAACP, said to Aunt Fannie Lou and the others who refused: "You all are ignorant. You don't understand politics. You all have won, why don't you accept whatever you can get and go back home? You've made the change; just learn to be realistic." Even at the prodding of Martin Luther King, Jr., Aunt Fannie Lou refused. Why should she accept two seats when other states had so many? To Aunt Fannie Lou that was still a defeat, and she rejected the compromise: "I came with nothing, I'll leave with nothing."

"You have to remember that at this time," Guyot said, "there was no Republican Party anywhere in the South. The real political power in the South was the Democratic Party, which, by seniority, controlled all of the major committees in the House and in the Senate. Our attempt at dealing with the impact of the Democratic Party had real national, state, regional and Southern ramifications. After Atlantic City, Fannie Lou Hamer was a political fireball. She was an active participant both in and outside the Democratic Party circles." In 1965, one of Aunt Fannie Lou's biggest accomplishments was the modification of the Voting Rights Act. "Fannie Lou Hamer, the Freedom Democratic Party and the Mississippi Movement did more to pass the Voting Rights Act than any other state," Guyot said. "The Voting Rights Act was the most effective piece of legislation ever written. We were a part of that modification, so Fannie Lou Hamer was an integral part of politics and everything the Freedom Democratic Party

did. She was not simply an observer, she was a prominent activist in both
the development of the plan and its implementation."

Aunt Fannie Lou continued to fight for what she believed in, including
better conditions in Mississippi; however, all of this work was beginning
to take its toll on her physically, mentally and emotionally. She was suffering from diabetes, heart disease and from the effects of the beating
she took in 1963. Reports indicate that she also suffered two nervous
breakdowns, one from nervous exhaustion and the other from the strain
of the load she was bearing. "That's clearly understandable," Guyot said.
"Fannie Lou Hamer was a very busy lady facing various kinds of opposition and the fight she was waging was an uphill one."
    During this very stressful time, one of Aunt Fannie Lou's biggest sup-
porters and good friend, Harry Belafonte, came to visit and financed a trip
for her and 11 others to Africa. "I had never been out of the country in my
life," Aunt Fannie Lou said earlier of the trip,"It was after the Convention
in 1964 and we needed the rest. That experience was life changing."
Coming from the heavily segregated South, Aunt Fannie Lou had never
seen a black stewardess on a plane, much less a black pilot. When she arrived in the Republic of Guinea, President Ahmed Sekou Toure was waiting for her. "It was just remarkable," she said. "After we got situated where
we were staying as guests of the government, the president was there, and
I met some of the most intelligent people. I had never in my life seen black
people running banks. I had never seen black people behind a counter in
a bank. I had never seen black people running the government; so it was
quite a revelation to me. I was really learning something for the first time.
And I could feel myself never, ever being ashamed of my ancestors and
my background." She said further, "I thought Sekou Toure was one of the
most fascinating guys I had ever met. When he would come in, whether it
was a man or a woman, he kissed them on each side. If a man would kiss a
man here (in Mississippi), he would hear all kinds of things. But they paid
no attention. I really was proud to see that kind of honesty in men sealing
their friendship. I loved it. I really loved every bit of it."

Following her trip to Africa and her exposure to the culture of her ancestors, Aunt Fannie Lou returned to Mississippi with a renewed strength and determination. At the same time, she was still physically tired and worn out. Despite her ill health, Aunt Fannie Lou continued to speak across the country and at nearly every major college campus in the nation. She organized grass roots and anti-poverty projects, school desegregation, child day care and low income housing. In 1968, she helped create a food cooperative to help the poor obtain more meat in their diet. In 1969, she started the Freedom Farm Cooperative in which 5,000 people were able to grow their own food and own 600 acres of land. And in 1972, she was a founding member of the National Women's Political Caucus.

Aunt Fannie Lou died on March 15, 1977, at the age of 59, from complications of her many ailments. Friends and family were quick to note that Aunt Fannie Lou's life's work had finally caught up with her. In fact, shortly before her death, Aunt Fannie Lou said, "People wouldn't have no idea how tired I would be."

When questioned early in her struggle as to whether or not she had faith that the system was working, Aunt Fannie Lou replied, "We have to make it work. Ain't nothing going to be handed to you on a silver platter. Nothing. You've got to fight. Every step of the way, you've got to fight."

Even after her death, Aunt Fannie Lou continued to impact the lives of others, personally and professionally. Her friend, Lawrence Guyot, states, "I continued to work to support her and her work. The civil rights movement was beginning to lapse around 1966. Now, did that mean that Fannie Lou Hamer's activities lapsed? No, but there was less public support and less coverage by the news. But she continued to impact everyone she ever met. It was hard for her not to be influential even if she tried not to be. I remember her as a principled woman who could not be frightened, manipulated or fooled. Fannie Lou Hamer was a religious fanatic, and I say that in the most positive frame of reference. Everything Fannie Lou Hamer did, regarding voting and empowering other people was based on her religious beliefs. She did everything she could to rid this world of discrimination, hunger, fear and the misuse of power. It is all so fantastic that Fannie Lou Hamer comes out of the black church."

My cousin Minnie, who attended the 1968 Democratic Convention in Chicago with Aunt Fannie Lou, also spoke of her dedication. Minnie said, "Going with her to Chicago was a great experience for me. She came out of the cotton fields and she didn't want to do that anymore because it was killing her. But it took a special kind of person to do what she [did]. I don't think I could have done it. And I'm so proud of her and who she was."

My mother agreed, noting the valuable lessons Aunt Fannie taught her and so many others. "Do things with your whole soul," Mary said. "That's what she did, and she did a lot for the state of Mississippi."

Now I understand and fully appreciate Fannie Lou Hamer—the person. Aunt Fannie Lou faced death constantly, and saw some of her closest friends and associates, namely, Andrew Goodman, Michael Schwerner, James Chaney, Medgar Evers, and Martin Luther King, Jr., killed; and yet she remained dedicated to her mission. Aunt Fannie Lou realized and often said that because of fierce racism and prejudice, Mississippi was at the bottom of the scale when it came to economic and educational achievements. Aunt Fannie Lou lived and died for change in the South, and unfortunately, more than 40 years later, statistically and nationally, Mississippi still lags behind every other state when it comes to economic and educational reform.

November 4, 2008, however, brought about the biggest change this country has ever seen with the election of the first black President of the United States of America. Without a doubt, Aunt Fannie Lou Hamer was a part of that process. In some respect, she was the reason for that success. Whatever, the case, I realize now that I also have a mission; that of preserving her memory and her struggle, and to remind people of the woman I came to know as Fannie Lou Hamer.

Mae Bertha Carter

"I am a grown woman who has birthed those
children and bore the pain and nobody can tell me
where to send my children to school."

Imagine living in the rural South, where beyond the eyes of the television cameras, racism was the most virulent, and civil rights workers were scarce. Mae Bertha Carter, standing alone, was determined to challenge the fear and intimidation rampant in her community even after passage of the Civil Rights Act of 1965. She would serve as a role model of empowerment through her actions and beliefs that education would lead to a better life for her children and for all underprivileged children.

Constance Curry

Constance Curry grew up in North Carolina, graduating from Agnes Scott College in Atlanta in 1955, and then studying abroad as a Fullbright Scholar. She was the first white woman appointed to the Student Non-Violent Coordinating Committee's Executive Board. She served as a field representative for the American Friends Service Committee from 1964 to 1975 and worked in Mississippi helping the Carter family and others in their efforts to desegregate the South. She served as Atlanta's Director of Human Services from 1975 to 1990. She has held fellowships at the University of Virginia's Center for Civil Rights and Emory University's Department of Women's Studies. She has a law degree from Woodrow Wilson College of Law. She currently lives and writes in Atlanta.

On a winter day in 1990, Mae Bertha Carter and Winson Hudson, both from Mississippi, were visiting me in Charlottesville, Virginia. They were to speak that morning at the University of Virginia in Julian Bond's class on the civil rights movement. I was there working on a post-doctoral fellowship at the Carter Woodson Institute to document the story of Mae Bertha Carter. Earlier in the year, I had met Maxwell Kennedy, the youngest son of Robert Kennedy, who was in law school at the University, and I had invited him to meet Mrs. Carter and Mrs. Hudson. They were so excited.

As with many black people in rural Mississippi, they saw in the 1960s, in both John and Robert Kennedy, the beginnings of recognition of, and caring about the blatant racism they faced on a daily basis. Just before Max Kennedy came, the two women disappeared in the back of the house. Max arrived and was sitting on the couch, and the two women came in. Embraces and introductions were exchanged, and then Mae Bertha and Winson sat down side by side on straight-back chairs—tiny, light-skinned, blue-eyed, 68 year-old Mae Bertha, and 74-year old tall, erect, strong-featured Winson Hudson—both from the back roads of Mississippi. They took out small pieces of paper and began to sing in clear, sure voices, the 1960s song, "Abraham, Martin and John." They changed the last verse to:

> Has anyone here seen my old friend Bobby?
> Can you tell me where he's gone?
> I thought I saw him walkin' up over the hill
> With Abraham, Martin and John.

Well, Max cried, I cried—we all cried, and I met Julian at his car, and told him what was happening inside, and he cried. I never dreamed that 12 years later, I would have completed books telling the stories of the lives of those two incredible women.

In 1964, I went to work for the American Friends Service Committee, as their Southern Field Representative. Beginning in 1960, I had been on the executive committee of the Student Nonviolent Coordinating Committee (SNCC)—the first white woman in those early years of SNCC—and AFSC wanted someone who knew the South and had worked with Movement people. They were anxious to help implement Title VI of the 1964 Civil Rights Act, mandating local school districts to come up with a school desegregation plan or risk losing federal funding for their schools. This would have been devastating for most rural schools, and the plan that many of them drafted was called "freedom of choice." It entailed informing all parents that they could select whatever school they wanted their child to attend in the district. A good plan on the surface, it was a snare and a delusion for the black families caught in the peonage of the sharecropping system.

Nonetheless, in Sunflower County, on a cotton plantation in the middle of the Mississippi Delta, Matthew and Mae Bertha made the decision in 1965 to send seven of their school-age children to the previously all-white schools in Drew, a small town nearby. The Carters had thirteen children in all, and the first five who attended the shamefully inadequate "colored" schools had left the Delta as soon as they graduated. Matthew and Mae Bertha never hesitated in the choice to get their remaining children a better education. The AFSC office was alerted to the ensuing intimidation and harassment that followed this choice, and I first went to visit the family in January of 1966. The previous fall, their house had been shot into, credit had been cut off, their crops were plowed under, they were being evicted, and their children were suffering terrible treatment from both teachers and students.

On that first visit, when I asked why they had made this choice, in light of the consequences for the whole family, Mae Bertha, in her eloquence told how she was tired of the worn out school books coming from the white schools and the raggedy school buses also handed down and black teachers who had no degrees. She told me, "Somebody had to do it." And when I asked Matthew the question about the "freedom" of choice, hands gently folded in his lap, he looked me right in the eye and said, "We thought they meant it." Certainly a tragic revelation of U.S. history that, in spite of a hundred years of broken promises, a black family in rural Mississippi would still believe.

Mae Bertha then told me about the overseer coming and trying to talk Matthew out of sending the children to the white schools and how she had sent the message back to him that she was a grown woman who had "birthed those children and bore the pain" and nobody could tell her where to send her children to school. She spoke of the embarrassments and persecution the seven children faced in the schools. First grader Deborah and third-grader Beverly were taunted and called names, including "walking tootsie roll." Pearl's fifth grade teacher had her sit in a desk isolated from the other children and had the white children rotate their seating so they would only have to sit by her one week at a time. And for high-schoolers Ruth, Larry, Stanley and Gloria, it was a constant barrage of name-calling, whites jumping aside from them when they passed in the hall, moving away from tables in the cafeteria as the Carters approached, to the point where the Carter children wouldn't even eat lunch. "We would just go outside and stand by the wall of the school." Joined by Carl, when he became of school age in 1967, they remained the only black children in the schools for five years, until Marian Wright Edelman filed suit in 1970. The suit asked for relief against a discriminatory system that placed a "cruel and intolerable burden on black parents and pupils."

As I noted in "Silver Rights" (p. xxiii) . . . "for the Carters and so many other families in the rural South, there were no federal troops to guard them and no reporters to tell the stories of their suffering. They not only faced danger from the white community but very often rejection by the black community as well. Abandoned by the federal government and forgotten by the American people, their children went to the white schools anyway."

I lost track of the Carters when I left the AFSC in 1975 and began to work for city government in Atlanta. Then in 1988, I saw Mae Bertha across the room at a conference on Women in the Civil Rights Movement.

We rushed to hug each other, and I asked about the family. She told me that Matthew had passed away earlier that year and that all of the children had graduated from the white schools, had gone on to college and that seven of them had graduated from the University of Mississippi. I was inspired to write and spent many hours with Mae Bertha in her living room in Drew, Mississippi interviewing her and all of the children. The result was "Silver Rights," published in 1995 by Algonquin Books of Chapel Hill. As noted in that book (p. 75) Mae Bertha's devotion to her children and her belief in the importance of education came down to her from her mother, Luvenia Noland Slaughter.

Mae Bertha Carter died in 1999, and a group of students approached the chancellor at the University of Mississippi and asked if a tree and a memorial plaque to Mae Bertha might be placed in the "circle" in front of the administration building. The "circle" was part of the area at "Ole Miss" where the riots occurred when James Meredith, the first black student, was admitted in 1962. The chancellor replied that only big donors and sports stars had trees planted for them in the "circle." The students replied that Mae Bertha and her family had given far more than that. In the fall, a red leaf maple tree was planted for her in the "circle" at "Ole Miss"—with a plaque in her memory—and to her seven children who graduated. Many of her thirteen children, thirty-six grandchildren and sixteen great grandchildren came to the ceremony and the little children helped dig the hole for the tree.

Gloria Dickerson

"I looked for some of my black friends but saw only
white faces with mean looks."

*Gloria Dickerson is a certified public accountant who received her bacher-
lor's degree in acocunting from the University of Mississippi in Oxford and
her MBA from Millsaps College in Jackson, Mississippi. She is the daughter
of Mae Bertha Carter who was highlighted in a biography, "Silver Rights,"
written by Constance Curry. Gloria Dickerson served as vice-president, finan-
cial operations for MIANC, Inc., in Jackson, Mississippi, and also served as
corporate controller for that company. She was an accountant with Northeast
Electric Power in Oxford, Mississippi and was named as Mid South Delta
Initiative Coordinator at the W. K. Kellogg Foundation. In this position,
Dickerson returns to her roots in Jackson, Mississippi, to help residents of
the Delta increase their opportunity for economic growth through the Mid
South Delta Initiative.*

I grew up in Sunflower County, deep in the Mississippi Delta, where picking cotton was the major way of making a living for poor black people. At the age of nine, I was picking and chopping cotton, often standing for hours in the hot sun daydreaming. Picking cotton was hard, backbreaking work and I would prick my fingers until they bled. Chopping cotton left me sweaty, my face often salty from perspiration. This was a miserable way to earn a living. My Mamma wanted a better life for all of her children. She said she was tired of seeing the white kids go to school while her children were in the cotton fields. Black kids did not go to school during the harvest season. The black schools were closed so the children could work in the fields. For the landowner, black kids working on the farm took priority over going to school. Mamma said she often cried because her children were being denied an education and she wanted that to change.

My brothers and sisters and I watched the bus coming toward us, the dust swirling in great circles as it sped down the dirt road. I was so excited and happy to be going to a good school. We were dressed in our finest clothes as we stood in the hot September sun eagerly waiting for the bus. I was a young child, my Mamma's words ringing in my ears: "Education will get you out of the cotton fields."

On that first day, climbing aboard a new shiny yellow bus, I was hopeful that other black children would be joining us. By the time we arrived at school, we were still the only ones. I looked for some of my black friends but did not see any. I saw only white faces with mean looks. I saw the stares as we entered the building. I felt the loneliness of being in a place that was very un-welcoming. I heard the word "niggers" over and over again. As I moved from one class to the next, I felt uneasy, and although the FBI, who had been assigned to protect us, reported that we were safe,

I did not feel safe that day or any other day, and neither did my sisters and brothers.

My siblings and I integrated the schools in Drew, Mississippi, in 1965 under the Freedom of Choice Plan, designed by the State of Mississippi to satisfy the requirements of the Civil Rights Act of 1965. We were the only black family in Sunflower County who chose to attend the all white school, a decision that could only fill my parents with agony, heartache and monumental terror. My mamma and my daddy were sending us off to school, Mamma believing in her "protective covering" and praying to her God to watch over her children.

The Civil Rights Act of 1965 forced the state of Mississippi to integrate the state's schools in order to continue to receive federal aid. Mississippi's plan was supposed to allow all parents, both black and white, to send their children to the school of their choice. My parents were determined to see their children educated. They wanted us to attend a good school, one with many books, modern equipment and decent buildings.

We were the Carters: Debra, Beverly, Pearl, Stanley, Larry, Ruth, and Gloria, the second "batch" of 13 children born to Mae Bertha and Matthew Carter. My Mamma and Daddy were sharecroppers in the Mississippi Delta who depended on the landowner and the plantation store to get food, supplies and medical care during the year. All of this was obtained on credit because the sharecroppers rarely had any money. At the end of the year, after the profit was determined, the landowner would settle up with the sharecropper. However, it was very common for sharecroppers to end the year in debt to the landowner. Thus, the cycle of dependency and poverty continued.

My sister, Pearl, recalls picking cotton and living in poverty. In 1963, our father earned seven dollars for one week's work. We had holes in our shoes. Apples, oranges, ketchup and soda were only available at special times. Indoor plumbing and running water became available when she was 10.

After my parents signed the Freedom of Choice papers to send us to the white school, word spread fast, and white folks were shocked! How dare my parents ask for such a thing! The next morning the plantation owner sent the manager to the house to tell my Daddy to withdraw his kids from the school. He even offered to go with my Daddy to the school for this purpose. However, after coaching from Mamma, Daddy told the manager NO, he was going to keep his children in the white school.

Can you imagine a black man in Mississippi in 1965 having the courage to tell his boss, a white man, NO? He said NO, and that NO brought consequences. The following night, after my Daddy told him NO, shots were fired into our house, the bullets going right over my head as I was sleeping. The next day after he said NO, my father was notified that he would not be able to buy food on credit. Shortly after he said NO, my Daddy came home and declared to my Mamma that he was catching hell everywhere he went. The plantation owner had given him an eviction notice, and he did not know where he was going to move his family, or for that matter, how he was going to feed them. The plantation owner told him that he did not make any money that year, and that Daddy actually owed him money after a year's work of hard labor on the farm.

Nineteen sixty five was a frightening time in Mississippi. It was a time when blacks were threatened, beaten, intimidated and lynched if they did not respond to the demands of the white majority. It was also a time when my parents were determined that they wanted to see change. My parents wanted their children to have a better life than they had as sharecroppers for over 30 years.

We children told Mamma and Daddy that we wanted to go to the white school. Mamma asked if we were sure and alerted us to the difficulties we might encounter. We wanted to take the chance; we were excited about the proposition of getting a good education that would lead to better jobs in the future.

As we traveled to school on the bus, I was hoping the driver would stop and pick up other black children before we got to school. At every stop he picked up white children who sat as far away from us as they could. Being first on the bus, we sat in the first four rows and the white children sat in the back. On the third day, when the bus driver picked us up, he told us to go to the back of the bus and never sit on the front seats again. He said that our place was in the back of the bus; I felt terribly humiliated.

When we reached school, I looked for my friends. I wanted so badly to see someone else who was black besides my sisters and brothers. Every class I went to on that first day, I looked for other black children. On the second and third day, I continued the search. Finally, realizing that no other black children were coming to Drew High School, I began to pray for just a friendly face. I wanted so badly for someone to be nice to me. Instead, I got the name calling and the spit balls; I went to school each day with apprehension about who would be mean to me. I was not welcome at school and all the white children let me know it. They told me that I was dumb and stupid and incapable of learning. They did not like the way I smelled. I felt the tension all around me. I was not wanted there and I felt like an outcast; I was lonely. It was only at the end of the day, when I arrived home, that I began to feel better.

We were not prepared for the onslaught of difficulties that awaited us. Debra, my six year old sister, was in first grade that September. None of the other kids was allowed to play with her. Debra remembers her teacher, Mrs. Drain, who would be her only play partner at recess. She recalls that black children would not play with the Carter children after school because their parents might have trouble with employers. Nobody talked to Beverly, my eight year old sister, who was in the third grade. The other kids talked about her and called her a "dirty nigger." Pearl, who was in the fifth grade that fall, had a teacher who constantly called her "stinky" and told her she "needed a bath." Pearl's teacher rotated the children in the class so that no child had to sit next to her all the time. For five long years, our faces burned with humiliation and shame, a time Pearl described as "years of hell." We never knew when we would be pushed, taunted or insulted by students or teachers. The punishment was relentless.

My Mamma prayed every day that the Good Lord would protect us and keep us safe. I'm sure praying brought comfort to Mamma but it didn't keep us safe. We were on our own terror alert every day. Mamma worried that one day we would not all come home from school. She said that for many weeks she would count her children, one by one, to make sure all of us got off the school bus. I did not feel safe at school or at home. I prayed every night for two things: one of my prayers was that the next day at school would be tolerable, that the kids would not be so mean and hostile. The other prayer to God was that He would not allow anybody to shoot into our house at night.

I always remember what my mamma said to me that encouraged me to get through the trials and tribulations of those days at school. Mamma would say: "No matter what they do or say to you, never say that you hate them. You should love those children as they are only saying the things their parents taught them. They have been taught to hate black children. You must love them in spite of what they say or do to you. They do not know any better, but you do: Jesus taught us to love one another."

Mamma had explained that the white adults try to preserve their way of life. They have always believed that black folks were less able than white folks. They think we should be their servants. They are trying to hold on to the past where the blacks would wait on or be subservient to the whites. That is why the white folks are so angry that blacks try to get a better education so they will get better jobs and appear to be more equal to the whites.

Mamma also taught us that the school is our school and that we have a right to be there. She told us to walk with pride and hold our heads up high. The whites are no better than we are, and we should not let them make us feel bad. She said the white children want us to think that we are inferior to them, but we are not. She also taught us that we were not better than the whites: we were all equal. "No person on this earth is superior to you," she would say. She reminded us that we were fighting for our rights, especially in the schools; nobody can take them away from us. She said, "Don't let them win. Don't ever accept second class citizenship. You have to love yourself; you have to love who you are."

I wanted so desperately to believe her and to feel good about myself and believe in myself; however, listening to others call me names and ridiculing me every day made it very difficult. Mamma's reinforcement was extremely helpful in keeping me motivated for my education. I trusted my parents and their encouragement more than the negative comments from my schoolmates. I knew I was fighting for my rights and that was very important.

My siblings and I endured being in this white school for five years. We continued to fight for justice and for what we believed was right. We were the only black family that chose to attend the all white school; we had courage, but we suffered as we fought for our rights.

After we realized that the Freedom of Choice Plan was not going to integrate the schools, Mamma filed a lawsuit against the Drew Public Schools claiming the Plan was causing the Carter children a cruel and intolerable burden and should be discarded. Our lawyer, Marian Wright Edelman, the first black female to pass the Mississippi Bar, won the lawsuit, and in 1969, 15 years after the *Brown vs. The Board of Education* decision, the schools in Mississippi were forced to integrate in a meaningful way.

I'm often asked was it worth it? Was it worth all the pain, suffering and loneliness that we endured? I feel that I have spent most of my life fighting to make things right, fighting for justice. A normally ordinary event, heading off to school, became an extraordinary event that September in 1965. The enormity of it all—the choice, the retaliation, the hatred, the fear—continues to haunt me to this day. Now that I am the mother of a son, I can only imagine the agony my parents felt as they put us on that school bus.

After high school and college, I was tired of fighting. Racism had taken its toll on me; I had spent more than five years of my life being punished for being black. I decided to stop fighting for justice and just live my life. No more civil rights or community meetings. No more agony and humiliation. By the time my son was in junior high school, the public schools had deteriorated academically and he was not getting the good education that my Mamma envisioned. Therefore, he went to a private Catholic school in order to obtain a better education. I did not want to fight any longer for improving or advocating for the public school system.

I have now come full circle and have taken up the fight for equality once more. Enduring all of the humiliation, hurt and pain at Drew High

School was just a moment in time. Your passion is where your pain is. That is a true statement because fighting for justice is what my life has been about. It was difficult to fight for the right to be educated. Now there are so many children living in poverty and I know that they do not have an equal opportunity to get a decent education. Thus, I struggle with what God has given me to continue to fight for others to be lifted from poverty the way I have been. Working with poor folks to help them love who they are is my current and future mission. Only when they feel free enough to attain a proper education will they be able to lift themselves out of poverty and into a better quality of life. This is the legacy of my parents, Mae Bertha and Matthew Carter.

Winson Hudson

"Oh come my dear children and sit by my knee,
and let me tell you the cost to be free.
If I don't tell you, you will never know,
Where you came from and where you should go."

*Winson Hudson, a founder of the NAACP Chapter in Harmony, MS., was a
leader in the civil rights movement in Mississippi, helping others register to
vote and leaving a legacy of commitment to the welfare of others. Her grandson, Kempton Horton, remembers details of her life and her positive influence
on him and others in the family.*

Postscript from a Grandson
Kempton Horton

Winson Hudson often stated that she walked down the halls of the legislative buildings in Washington, D.C., lobbying for the needs of the poor but never wore a cap and gown! I knew her as one who was gentle as a lamb but could be fierce when provoked. My grandmother, who raised my mother, my brother and me contributed to the characteristics and qualities I am most proud of today. While feared by some, she was respected by all. I have learned the ways of life through her teachings.

My grandmother was born Winson Gates in Harmony, Mississippi, on November 17, 1916. She lived at a time when lynchings were on the rise, the Ku Klux Klan had returned to power and trade unions denied membership to skilled black artisans. She also lived at a time when W. E. B. DuBois developed a foundation on which Martin Luther King could build his dream. She was the tenth of thirteen children born to John Wesley Gates and Emma Kirkland. As with most blacks in the South at that time, neither of her parents had ever considered registering to vote. Grandma's mother died when grandma was eight years of age and she and her siblings were raised by her father, my great grandfather, on a 100 plus acre farm that was later confiscated by a physician to whom the family owed money. Winson married Cleo Hudson in 1936. His family also owned property in Harmony, which had been the center for black property owners since the Civil War.

Grandma had a very close relationship with her sister, Dovie, my great aunt. Aunt Dovie and Grandma lived about a quarter of a mile from each other. Every Saturday, we would stop by to pick up Aunt Dovie, who would ride with us to the city limits of Carthage to shop and to socialize. I think going to Carthage was a way for her to get some time to herself. Dovie went with Grandma everywhere—they were a dynamic duo. Grandma would make sure that Dovie and family were OK, and Dovie would do the same for Grandma. I can remember both sisters shopping together for clothing. They always shopped at Sears and Roebuck or Lane Bryant's. Grandma said those stores were for stout women like her and Aunt Dovie. If she would buy a particular dress or blouse, Aunt Dovie would get the same, but in an different color.

I can also remember on Saturday mornings, during the summer months, the families helping each other in the gardens. A garden was something that seemed to soothe the two women. My mom also enjoyed the pleasure of working in the gardens, but my brother and I hated that work. We did, however, love the products of our labors, including the vegetables that Grandma would often share with friends and others. Sometimes I wondered why we would pick vegetables just to give them away, but later learned that was Grandma teaching us the gift of giving.

I guess she was an average cook, but probably a better cook than we gave her credit for being. I only say that because not many people today can make homemade biscuits and tea cakes the way she did. Grandma had a few favorite dishes. She loved homemade biscuits, grapefruit, black eyed peas, cornbread and cornflakes. She often told us that as a child, she could not get enough cornflakes and she was going to eat them as often as she could once she could afford to do so.

My grandmother also had a strong relationship with the public. People gravitated toward her. Within the city limits of Carthage, people knew her well and wanted to talk to her and tell their personal business. It seemed as though she would listen forever; then—she would give advice to the neighbor. My grandmother was more like a mother and a counselor to the public. As an example of her humility, she would take care of the needs of others before she cared for her own.

Civil Rights Activities

Grandma Winson told me that her grandmother, Angeline, had been a slave. She was shipped to Mississippi at three years of age from Alabama. She was freed following the Civil War and had nowhere to go. She worked for a white family and had two children by two of the sons of the family. Angeline told my grandmother about slavery and to stay away from white people. "She didn't like the way whites treated slaves." Grandma Winson told me that she took her strength from her father, "who made me brave." She said, "He wasn't afraid and made all us kids brave." Her father was a minister who became mother and father to the family when Winson's mother died.

Grandma Winson worked as a teacher and demonstrated her civil rights interest early by providing bread for hungry children from the lunchroom that she managed. She recognized the dangers of working in civil rights and believed that she could do more than a man could do, because the danger was greater for men than for women. Grandma Winson initially tried to register to vote in 1937, when she was 21 years of age. It took her 25 years, until 1962, when she finally succeeded.

Grandma had been told that she had not sufficiently interpreted sections of the Mississippi constitution allowing her to pass the voter registration test. In 1962 she answered the registrar's questions regarding the meaning of a particular passage by saying, "It said what it meant and it meant what it said." She passed the exam and with great pride took her place at the polls as a registered voter of the State of Mississippi.

In 1961, one year prior to her success in registering to vote, she and her sister, Dovie, prayed in the basement of the courthouse not to be killed by the whites who were blocking their way in their attempt to register to vote. I can remember Grandma saying that Dovie prayed for them everywhere they went. Aunt Dovie prayed that day for a shield to protect them. At that time, Grandma was given a card with red eyes stating, "The eyes of the Klan are upon you—you have been identified by the White Knights of the Ku Klux Klan." She said to me, "We were facing death."

When the Voting Rights Act of 1965 became law, Grandma Winson led a drive that resulted in 500 black voters in Leake County in one year. She became heavily involved in school politics and worked diligently as a field secretary for the NAACP, the organization that gave her the strength and the opportunity to succeed in her mission to help poor blacks in the South. Her life really centered around the cause of the NAACP. This organization gave her wings and fueled her fire. At that time, my brother, Donovan, and I could not understand why my grandmother was working so hard, but we later understood that it was her passion.

Grandma Winson and Great Aunt Dovie were instrumental in filing a lawsuit in 1961 to integrate the schools countywide. It took three years, until 1964, when a federal court ordered desegregation. She told me, "I wouldn't back down from anything" even after her house and Dovie's house were bombed in the early 1960s. She told me that a number of people had told her that she was headed for trouble if she continued her civil rights activism. That not only provided Grandma with greater incentive, as she said, "If I don't do it, who will."

Grandma's involvement with civil rights was deep. She had a passion for what she believed. Answers to problems just seemed to roll off her tongue. There were times when she would stay on the telephone for long periods of time trying to help someone get a loved one out of jail or just talking about how to increase membership in the NAACP.

Grandma's philosophy was that she had "the love of God in my heart." She said, "I have helped some people and never took money from them." She said she had known Medgar Evers before civil rights. She found him to be a good man who was not afraid of anyone, yet knew the danger of his work would lead to his untimely death. She also talked about her relationship with Fannie Lou Hamer and Annie Devine. Her advice for young people, whom she considered greatly, was to stop and listen to old people before it's too late. She recounted the hard time that she and others had experienced and was concerned that the youngsters are now "taking for granted." Her concern for the youth was expressed through a poem she had written and was proud to share with all who would listen.

> Oh come my dear children and sit by my knee,
> And let me tell you the cost to be free.
> If I don't tell you, you will never know,
> Where you came from and where you should go.
> You contributed more than any race in this nation
> Coming through hard trials and tribulation,
> Fought in every war in American's name,
> You never have dragged her flag to shame.
> You can't afford to wait another day.

If I don't tell you, you will never know,
Where you came from and where you should go.

I never really knew how my grandmother could relax with all of the events going on around her. After she retired from Head Start, she would continue to get up at about 6:30 a.m. I often thought of Grandma Winson as a super grandmother. I wondered how she had time for the public and could still come home and enjoy her family. I had a passion for comedy, so I would keep her laughing with what was going on in society. We would joke about how things have changed and how young kids wore their clothes. Grandma said if we had a job interview to dress appropriately. She said boys should not wear earrings and they should make sure their pants were rolled up. I felt like I had the best life coach a person could ask for. Grandma said, "Don't be too proud" and "always help people." She would often say, "God don't like ugly, so be courteous to people." She would often tell my brother and me to respect people and never steal anything from anybody. She said if there was something we wanted, we should work hard for it. She stated that prospective employers would place money in a specific area to see if it would be taken. This was a test that the employers used to see the applicants were honest. I feel that my grandmother had a big influence on my life. She is responsible for me and my brother being the men we are today. I am very grateful for that.

Constance Curry, noted author, attorney and former field representative for the American Friends Service Committee, states that she had been contacted by Winson Hudson in the year 2000 to help her finish her book. According to Ms. Curry, Ms. Hudson was losing her sight, was unable to walk and wanted to hold the book in her hands before she died. Her goal was accomplished. Ms. Hudson was able to hold the book, *Mississippi Harmony, Memoirs of A Freedom Fighter*,[1] in her hands before she passed away.

Grandma Winson, who was known by many for her refusal to be

---

1 Mississippi Harmony, Memoirs of a Freedom Fighter, Talgrave/McMillan, 2002.

intimidated, died on April 24, 2004, at the age of 87. Her contributions to the country were finally recognized in a half-page obituary in the New York Times, dated Sunday, May 9, 2004. According to Vernon E. Jordan, Jr., a colleague at the NAACP: "Mrs. Hudson was one of the unsung, unheralded heroes of the civil rights movement." Further, he stated, "Her work represented the essence of what took place. There is a lot written about the leaders but not much about the contribution of the Mrs. Hudsons of the world." Bob Moses, Field Secretary of SNCC in Mississippi in the 1960s, also contributed to the obituary stating, "It is inconceivable that the Movement could have happened the way it did in Mississippi without Mrs. Hudson."

Finally, the obituary noted, "Her legacy is marked by Hudson Road, which runs near her house. It is fitting to have the road named after her since she was instrumental in having the roads in Harmony, Mississippi, a rural community, finally paved."

Hazel Brannon Smith

Remembering A Great Lady of American Journalism

"If ever the martyrs to a free press in America
assembled in Heaven, there is one thing I know:
Hazel Brannon Smith will be in the front rank."

*Hazel Brannon Smith was the owner and editor of four weekly newspapers in rural
Mississippi and was the first woman to receive the Pulitzer Prize for Editorial Writing.
Her editorials in her column ("Through Hazel Eyes") focused on unpopular causes, po-
litical corruption and social injustice in Mississippi. She also received awards from the
National Federation of Press Women, the Herrick Award for Editorial Writing, the
Mississippi Press Association. She was president of the International Society of Weekly
Newspaper Editors from 1981 to 1982. In 1954, when the local sheriff shot a young
black man in the back, Mrs. Smith wrote in a front page editorial in The Advertiser
that the sheriff had violated "every concept of justice, decency and right." As a result of
her stance, Mrs. Smith's newspaper became the target of an economic boycott, and the
Segregationist White Citizens Council started an opposition paper. The boycott lasted
10 years, drained Mrs. Smith financially and eventually forced The Advertiser to close.
But she continued to speak out against racism and bigotry.*

Bill Minor

*Bill Minor grew up in Southeast Louisiana, graduating from Tulane University in 1943
with a degree in journalism. He is a World War II Naval Combat Veteran. He was
journalist for the Times-Picayune in New Orleans as the Mississippi correspondent, a
post he held for 30 years, covering the violent civil rights era. When he retired from
the newspaper in 1976, he stayed in Jackson, Mississippi, and became a statewide syn-
dicated political columnist. Minor has won numerous awards, among them in 1966,
the Louis Lyons Award given by the Nieman Foundation at Harvard University for
"Conscience and Integrity in Journalism." He was installed in the Hall of Fame of the
Mississippi Press Association in 1991. In 1997, he became the first recipient of the John
Chancellor Award for Excellence in Journalism, presented by the Annenberg School of
Communications at the University of Pennsylvania. This chapter is his eulogy at the
funeral for Hazel Brannon Smith.*

If I could preserve a snapshot in time of how I would prefer to remember Hazel, it would be of a high-spirited, strikingly attractive woman editor I saw floating regally through the once-luxurious lobby of Biloxi's Buena Vista Hotel at the Mississippi Press Convention, turning the heads of a dozen editors as she went.

Or a snapshot of a joyful, smiling Southern gal in a Hattie Carnegie hat occupying the center of attention from the leading state politicians who came to socialize with the gathering of Mississippi newspaper people.

Or of a radiant Hazel driving off in her white Cadillac convertible seemingly without a care in the world to take off on still another trip to San Francisco or New York, then to some foreign land.

Or of Hazel as a delegate to the Democratic National Convention in 1940 when Damon Runyon described her as the prettiest delegate in the convention.

Those were snapshots of the happier days in the lifetime of Hazel Brannon when she played to the hilt the role of a flamboyant country newspaper editor, envied by all who knew her for her spunk, audacity and brains. Many were her male admirers who were crushed when Hazel returned from a world tour in the early 1950s with her husband-to-be, Walter Dyer Smith–her dear Smitty—whom she had met on her cruise.

But the Southern gentlemen who took this fetching belle for helpless in those years soon found out how mistaken they were if they thought she would not take a tough editorial stand in her newspaper. Once, Hazel told an interviewer for a national magazine: "I ain't no lady . . . I'm a newspaperwoman."

Driven by a strong Christian conscience, a keen sense of justice and liberty and a compassion for the underdog, that is the hallmark of American journalism. Hazel inevitably was drawn to oppose racial intolerance, a stand that originally was not popular in Mississippi in the 1950s and 1960s. In fact, it was fraught with great personal risks, not the least of which was the threat to economic survival.

But Hazel took her stand to oppose the racial bigots, even when they organized the county power structure to choke off the newspaper's economic sustenance and a campaign of harassment in an effort to throttle her editorial voice. Hazel was at her best when she took on the organized wrath of the hate mongers who were determined to drive her out of business.

Against great odds, she held on and fought back, somehow keeping her *Lexington Advertiser* and the *Durant* afloat. Her peers in the profession of journalism nationally at last recognized her in 1964 by awarding her the Pulitzer Prize for her courageous editorial stand.

Thomas Jefferson, the architect of the First Amendment and its commitment to the concept of the freedom of the press, the cornerstone of American Journalism, wrote in 1799: *To preserve the freedom of the human mind . . . and the freedom of the press, every spirit should be ready to devote itself to martyrdom."*

Hazel, this Alabama girl who loved the University of Alabama, and worshiped Bear Bryant, was transplanted to Mississippi by fate, and touched by the spirit of liberty of which Thomas Jefferson spoke.

If ever the martyrs to a free press in America assembled in Heaven, there is one thing I know: Hazel Brannon Smith will be in the front rank.

Afterword

In order to fully understand the major impact of civil rights in the United States in the Twentieth Century, it is useful to put relevant historical events in a meaningful temporal position. Thus, we have included a timeline placing the events leading to the civil rights movement, that resulted in *de facto* equality for all citizens of the United States. Legislation and Supreme Court decisions were helpful, but were often violated by citizens of the Southern states who resented the imposition of the rest of the country on their economy, their morality and their utilization of slaves and later exploitation of minority citizens. This timeline highlights the important events, placing them in context that will help the reader understand the dangers of pursuing the civil rights movement at the time and in the place where it was most needed: in Mississippi and other Southern states during the 1960s. The heroic acts of these courageous women depicted in "Pieces from the Past" were instrumental in paving the way for black citizens to vote and to hold office. When Barack Obama became President of the United States, he stood on some powerful shoulders, both men and women, who understood the passion and importance of the great political and moral questions of our time: the civil rights of all citizens.

Historical Timeline

Women in Civil Rights

19th Century

1890   Emma Frances Grayson Merritt starts first U.S. kindergarten for African American children.

1891   Lucy Parsons founded the newspaper: "Freedom: A Revolutionary Anarchist Communist Monthly."

1892   Anna Julia Cooper published "Voice of the South" about the status of African-American women.

————   Hallie Brown "Lady principal" (dean at Tuskegee Institute).

————   Patent for ironing board invented by Sarah Boone.

1894   National Association of Colored Women began publishing The Women's Era.

1895   National Federation of Afro-American Women founded by about 100 women from ten states.

1897   Phyllis Wheatley Home for Aged Colored Ladies founded by Fannie M. Richards in Detroit.

20th Century

1902   Local white protests of the appointment of Minnie Cos as postmistress of Indianola, Mississippi, led to President Theodore Roosevelt suspending postal service to the town.

1903   Maggie Lena Walker founded St. Luke's Penny Savings Bank in Richmond, Virginia, becoming the first woman bank president.

—— Sara Breedlove Walker (Madam C. J. Walker) began her hair care business.

1904 Mary McLeod Bethune founded Bethune Cookman College.

1907 Negro Rural School Fund established by Anna Jeans for purpose of improving education for rural southern African Americans.

1908 Woman's Day Nursery Association formed to provide care for African American children whose mothers worked outside the home.

1911 Forerunner of the National Urban League formed.

1913 Rosa Parks born.

1918 Frances Elliot Davis enrolled with the American Red Cross, the first African-American to do so.

1919 Mary White Ovington becomes the first chairperson of the NAACP.

1921 Bessie Coleman becomes the first African-American to earn a pilot's license.

—— Three African American women earn Ph.D. degrees; Georgiana Simpson, University of Chicago; Sadie T. Mossell Alexander, University of Pennsylvania; Eva Dykes, Radcliffe.

1923 Bessie Smith records "Down Hearted Blues."

—— Cotton Club opened in Harlem and only women whose skin color was lighter than a brown paper bag were hired.

1932 Augusta Savage started the largest art center in the U.S., Savage Studio of Arts and Crafts in New York.

1933 The Civilian Conservation Corp employs 250,000 African American women and men.

1935 National Council of Negro Women founded.

1936 Mary McLeod Bethune appointed by FDR to National Youth Administration.

1938 Crystal Bird Faust elected to Pennsylvania House of Representatives.

—— Virginia Foster Durr helps found the Southern Conference for Human Welfare, which later became the National Committee to Abolish the Poll Tax.

1939   Jane Matilda Bolin appointed justice of Domestic Relations Court of New York, becoming the first African American woman judge.

——   Hattie McDaniel wins Best Supporting Actress Oscar, the first African American to do so.

——   Marian Anderson denied permission to sing at DAR hall. Eleanor Roosevelt resigns in protest.

——   Ella Baker becomes a field organizer for the NAACP.

1950   Althea Gibson plays at Wimbledon.

——   Juanita Hall, first African American to win a Tony for her role as Bloody Mary in "South Pacific."

1956   Rosa Parks arrested for refusing to give up her seat on the bus to a white man.

——   Ella Baker, Bayard Rustin and Stanley Levinson meet with Martin Luther King, Jr., leading to founding of SCLC one year later.

——   Septima Poinsette Clark becomes vice president of Charleston NAACP and develops "citizenship Schools" to teach literacy.

1957   Althea Gibson wins Wimbledon and the U.S. Open; the AP names her "Woman Athlete of the Year."

1959   "Raisin in the Sun" becomes the first Broadway play written by an African American woman, Lorraine Hansberry.

1960   Ruby Bridges integrates an all-white school in New Orleans.

1963   Four young black girls were killed in a church bombing in Birmingham, Alabama, reaching national attention and prompting further activists to come to the South to help the black and white members of Student Nonviolent Coordinating Committee (SNCC) help blacks achieve the right to vote.

1964   Fannie Lou Hamer testifies for the Mississippi Freedom Democratic Party before the Democratic National Committee.

1965   Patricia Harris becomes the first African American ambassador to Luxemburg.

——   Viola Gregg Luizzo murdered by an Alabama Klu Klux Klan member.

1966   Constance Baker Motley appointed the first black female federal judge.

1968   Shirley Chisholm elected to the U.S. House of Representatives and becomes the first African American woman to run for President of the United States.

1972   Barbara Jordan elected to the U.S. House of Representatives.

1976   Barbara Jordan gives the keynote address at the Democratic National Convention.

1977   Pauli Murray becomes first black female Episcopal priest.

1978   Faye Wattleton becomes president of Planned Parenthood.

1979   Hazel Winifred Johnson becomes the first black female general.

1983   "The Color Purple" wins the National Book Award and the Pulitzer Prize.

——   Toni Morrison wins the Nobel Prize for Literature.

1988   Florence Griffith Joyner wins four medals in the Olympics.

1989   Oprah Winfrey creates Harpo Productions.

1990   Sharon Pratt Kelly elected mayor of Washington, D.C.

——   Roselyn Payne Epps becomes first black female president of the AMA.

1992   Mae Jemison becomes first black female in space.

1993   Joycelyn Elders becomes first black female U.S. Surgeon General.

1995   Ruth Simmons becomes first black president of Smith College.

1998   DNA evidence confirms theory that Thomas Jefferson fathered Sally Hemings' children.

21st Century

2000   Condoleeza Rice named Secretary of State.

2001   Ruth Simmons becomes the president of Brown University.

2002   Halle Berry becomes the first African American woman to win the Best Actress Oscar.

2003   The bus made famous by Rosa Parks is added to the Henry Ford Museum in Michigan.

2010   Dorothy Height dies. She led the National Council of Negro Women and marched with Dr. Martin Luther King, Jr.

Source of information for this Timeline is http://womenhistoryabout.com

Acknowledgments

I am deeply indebted to my husband, Bob, for his support, encouragement and willingness to participate in the Mississippi project. In many ways, he exemplifies the attributes of the heroes in this book. He has devoted his personal and professional life to protecting the rights of others and to giving voice to those unheard. Without his inspiration and dedication, this book would not have been written.

Linda Needleman, friend, confidant, colleague and co-editor, has worked diligently editing, correcting and improving the quality of this book. In addition to her professionalism and editorial skills, Linda has been a major support throughout this experience. I will always be grateful to her on so many levels.

Special thanks to:

Laura Lipson, Director, "Standing on My Sisters' Shoulders", friend, colleague and companion in making dreams come true.

Ruth Shultz, who took the time to read the entire manuscript and provide meaningful feedback which has been essential to the completion of this book.

William Ferris, Ph.D., advisor and friend, currently Director, Center for the Study of the American South, the University of North Carolina, Chapel Hill.

Walter Biggins, Acquisitions Editor, University Press of Mississippi, who asked the questions and pushed for more.

Barbara Meil, who encouraged me to take the essential next step in producing our first film, "Philadelphia, Mississippi: Untold Stories".

Marilyn Lager, Librarian, Friends' Central School, Wynnewood, Pennsylvania, for her continuing source of strength, encouragement and friendship.

Julie Sadoff, J.D., Ph.D., whose wisdom and expertise I deeply respect. Her editorial skills improved the final version of this book.

Rachel C. Sadoff for her creativity and technical contributions to this project.

Melissa Vuernick, mentor, advisor and friend.

"Pieces From the Past" would not have been possible without the commitment and devotion of Ruth Borock, whose endless support, dedication and willingness to type and retype the contents of this book, made the process so much easier for me.

To my family and friends, I thank you for being there and listening to the never ending saga of "The Book".

Finally, I am forever indebted to the women whose courage and commitment to the cause of freedom provided these "Pieces From the Past".

Bibliography

Angelo, Maya, *I Know Why the Caged Bird Sings*: Random House, New York, 1969.

Curry, Constance, *Deep in Our Hearts: Nine White Women in the Freedom Movement*: University of Georgia Press, Atlanta, October 20, 2000.

Curry, Constance, *Silver Rights*: Algonquin Books of Chapel Hill, Chapel Hill, North Carolina, 1995.

Curry, Constance; *Mississippi Harmony: Memories of a Freedom Fighter*: McMillan, New York, 2002.

Hine, Darlene Clark, *Black Women in America: A Historical Encyclopedia*: Carlson Publishing Inc., Brooklyn, New York, 2003.

Mars, Florence, *Witness in Philadelphia*; Louisiana State University Press, Baton Rouge, 1977.

Mills, Kay, *This Little Light of Mine: The Life of Fannie Lou Hamer*; Dutton Press, Hialeah, Fl, 1994.

Moody, Ann, *Coming of Age in Mississippi*; Laurel Books: Dell Publishing Company, New York, 1968.

Morris, Joanne Prichard, *Barefootin': Life Lessons from the Road to Freedom* (with Unita Blackwell); Crown Press, Phoenix, Arizona, 2006.

Robinson, JoAnn Gibson, *The Montgomery Bus Boycott and the Women Who Started it: The Memoir of JoAnn Gibson Robinson*: University of Tennessee Press, Knoxville, 1987.

Walker, Alice, *In Search of our Mothers' Gardens*: Harcourt Brace, San Diego, New York, 1967.

DVD

Lipson, Laura, Director, *Standing on my Sisters' Shoulders*; Distributed by Women Make Movies, New York, 2001.

Selected Quotes

"Pieces from the Past"

"America, you got to think about your soul."—Annie Devine ("Standing on My Sisters' Shoulders"—DVD)

"I came of age during the revolution, a bloody and painful revolution which left physical and spiritual scars on a generation of Americans that are now only beginning to heal."—Constance Slaughter Harvey

"The ballot is perhaps the most powerful weapon to bring to a diversified society."—Constance Slaughter Harvey

"What were we trying to change?—Everything."—Joan Mulholland

"I'm going to be free or continue to be part of a struggle to fight for the freedom of people in this country."—June Elizabeth Johnson

"If I die, I die for somethin'."—Unita Blackwell ("Standing on My Sisters' Shoulders"—DVD)

"If one southern family can change this much, surely there is hope for the larger society."—Betty Pearson

"The only thing they could do was kill me—they've been trying a little bit at a time ever since I could remember."—Fannie Lou Hamer

"I'm sick and tired of being sick and tired."—Fannie Lou Hamer ("Standing on My Sisters' Shoulders"—DVD)

"I looked for some of my black friends but saw only white faces with mean looks."—Gloria Dickerson

"I wonder when are people going to learn color don't have anything to do with it. People are people."—Mae Bertha Carter ("Silver Rights")

"We felt like we had to break the cycle."—Mae Bertha Carter (N.Y. Times, Jan. 28, 1996)

"The eyes of the Klan are upon you"—"We were facing death."—Winson Hudson

"I ain't no lady—I'm a newspaper woman."—Hazel Brannon Smith

About the Editors

Joan H. Sadoff, MEd., MSW, Editor. As a clinical social worker and lecturer, she has worked in hospital, family agency and community settings. Listed in "Who's Who in Mental Health," she has lectured nationally and internationally on the Impact of Societal Change on the Family. Ms. Sadoff is the recipient of numerous awards, including recognition by Temple University in their "Gallery of Success" and was selected Social Worker of the Year (2005) by the National Association of Social Workers (NASW) for the State of Pennsylvania. She is currently involved in the production of documentary films focusing on civil rights and the South, including the award-winning film, "Standing on My Sisters' Shoulders." "Pieces from the Past" is her first published book.

Robert L. Sadoff, M.D., Co-Editor, is currently Clinical Professor of Forensic Psychiatry and Director of the Forensic Psychiatry Fellowship Program at the University of Pennsylvania, Philadelphia, Pa. He has been in the private practice of forensic psychiatry for almost 50 years and has received a number of national and international awards for his work in forensic psychiatry. He has published over 100 professional papers and 30 chapters in other people's books. This is his 10th published book.

Linda Needleman, M.Ed., Co-Editor, worked as a teacher of gifted children in the Philadelphia Public School System for nearly 30 years. She developed and taught the curriculum "From the Cold War to the Cola Wars," an elective in post World War II history, with a focus on civil rights. Since retiring from full time teaching she has worked as a freelance editor and works as an adjunct professor at Chestnut Hill College, Philadelphia.